TRUE

Being true to yourself, your
God, your relationships

Sarah Bradley

True: Being true to yourself, your God, your relationships

© Sarah Bradley / The Good Book Company 2011

Reprinted 2012, 2013

The Good Book Company
Blenheim House, 1 Blenheim Road, Epsom, Surrey, KT19 9AP, UK.
Tel: 0333-123-0880; International: +44 (0) 208 942 0880
Email: admin@thegoodbook.co.uk

Websites:
UK: www.thegoodbook.co.uk
North America: www.thegoodbook.com
Australia: www.thegoodbook.com.au
New Zealand: www.thegoodbook.co.nz

ISBN: 9781909559356

Design and illustration: André Parker
Printed and bound by CPI Group (UK) Ltd, Croydon, CR0 4YY

Contents

1 Be true to yourself   5
Your relationship with yourself

2 The one true God   17
Your relationship with God

3 Your true family   33
Your relationship with church

4 True friendship   47
*Your relationships with your
friends*

5 Home truths   61
*Your relationship with your
parents*

6 True love   75
Your relationships with boys

7 Truth or dare   91
*Your relationships with
non-Christians*

8 It's tough being true   105
Your relationship with the world

Final thoughts   119

1. Be true to yourself

Your relationship with yourself

When I was ten, my friend, Sarah, was tall, slim, ladylike, and looked like a ballerina. Her beautiful, narrow feet meant she could wear lovely, dainty shoes and look really pretty. Sarah means "princess"—and my friend was just like a princess.

I'm called Sarah too. But I was average height, average weight, and not at all ladylike. I had one of the widest pairs of feet in my class (including the boys!). My shoes weren't delicate or beautiful. I longed to have lovely, narrow feet like Sarah. Sadly, it never happened!

Have you ever compared yourself to someone and thought you're not as good, or clever, or pretty (or thin, sporty, musical, arty…) as them? It's easy to do, isn't it? You might compare yourself with your sister or brother, or a friend at school. Or there's a celebrity you'd love to be like. Often we compare ourselves to others and the result isn't good—because it leaves us unhappy. We feel we're not as good as them, and never will be.

Or maybe it's the opposite. Maybe you have a great opinion of yourself. You know you're the best at netball or basketball, or in the top class for everything, or really good at music or art. So you look down your nose at other people and think: "I'm so much better than them".

At some point in our lives we're likely to do one or the other. Maybe even both. You may be brilliant at something, but still look at someone else and wish you had her hair, or could sing as well as her.

We can be very quick to compare ourselves to other people—and often it leaves us sad and unsatisfied with who we are.

The biggest worry

I wonder what your biggest worry is. What do you worry about the most?

Maybe it's your weight. You think you're too fat or too skinny, and you look at other people and wish you could look like them.

Maybe it's your clothes. You think other people have cooler or more expensive clothes than you, or look better in them. Or you think: "If I could just have this coat, or that top, or that necklace, then I'd be happy".

Perhaps it's your looks. You think you'd be happier with lighter or darker hair, a different body shape, longer legs, a flatter stomach.

Maybe it's your talents. You wish you could dance, sing, or play sport like someone else. Or you long to be cleverer, funnier, more interesting.

Perhaps it's boys. Your friends have boys interested in them and you don't. Or a boy who is interested in you is one you don't like—but the boy you do like doesn't even talk to you. (We'll look more at this in chapter 6.)

Amy's story

Let me tell you about Amy Carmichael:

Amy Carmichael was born in Ireland, in 1867. There was something she wasn't happy with—she had brown eyes, but wanted them to be blue. When she was a little girl, she dreamed of having blue eyes. She often asked God to make her brown eyes blue, ***but it never happened***.

Years later, Amy became a missionary in India. Sometimes she rescued girls who were sold to Hindu temples as slaves. It was when she became a missionary that she understood why God had always said no to her prayer. Even though she wasn't Indian, her brown eyes meant she could move among the Indian people without being seen as something different, because they had brown eyes too. With blue eyes she would have stood out too much!

God created Amy exactly the way she should be. He knew His future plans for her—He knew what she would be doing and where she would be doing it. God thought about and planned all the details, even the colour of her eyes. ***God plans and prepares everything***, and He knows what's best for each one of us.

A song about God

King David was a great king who lived for God. He wrote Psalm 139—a song that reminds us that God knows everything that's happening, and there's nowhere in the world that He isn't King.

We can read what David says about God in verses 13-16:

For you created my inmost being;
you knit me together in my mother's womb.
I praise you because I am fearfully and wonderfully made;
your works are wonderful,
I know that full well.
My frame was not hidden from you
when I was made in the secret place.
When I was woven together in the depths of the earth,
your eyes saw my unformed body.
All the days ordained for me
were written in your book
before one of them came to be.

Psalm 139 v 13-16

Do you sometimes think: "What on earth am I here for? What's the point of me?" Psalm 139 says that God "knit you together in your mother's womb". He created you and planned you. He knew what you'd look like, what you'd be good at, the things you'd do, the places you'd go. **He knew why He was putting you here.**

Because God loves you so much, He's planned all this! It's brilliant to know that you're who and what you are for a reason. God made you as you are, because that's how He wanted you to be. He has plans for you and thinks you're special. Amy didn't realise this to begin with, but later she learned why God had given her brown eyes. Like Amy, God wants you to continue to grow in your love, trust and obedience to Him.

Maybe you don't understand why you are the way you are. But look again at what God says in verse 14: you are "fearfully and wonderfully made". God's works are wonderful. He doesn't make mistakes.

This is really important. If we don't understand and believe this, it can have serious consequences.

If we compare ourselves to others—or if we think that what we look like, or are good at, is the most important thing about us—we'll always end up disappointed. **That's not what God wants for us, and it's not how God sees us.**

God chooses us

God isn't a sports captain, or magazine editor, or judge on a TV talent show. God doesn't look at His world and think: "There's someone beautiful; I'll let her be a Christian," or "There's someone with a great singing voice; she'll make a good Christian". Or even "There's someone good and well-behaved; she'll make a good Christian".

Read what we're told in the book of Ephesians. If you're a Christian, this is true for you...

For he [God] chose us in him before the creation of the world to be holy and blameless in his sight.

In love he predestined us [decided long ago] to be adopted as his sons through Jesus Christ, in accordance with his pleasure and will—to the praise of his glorious grace, which he has freely given us in the One he loves.

Ephesians 1 v 4-6

These verses say that if you're a Christian, you were chosen before the world was created. Before anything was here, God had chosen you to be part of His kingdom!

Why?

It doesn't say He chose us to be beautiful or talented or popular—but to be "holy and blameless". God chose you to be adopted into His family; to become more like Him. If you're a Christian, you're already in; you're already a child of God—in "accordance with His pleasure and will". That means He wanted to do it, and He enjoyed doing it. God, the Creator of the whole world, wanted to adopt you, and wants you to become holy and blameless. **That's what matters to Him.**

If you wouldn't call yourself a Christian, God wants you to know this too. Why not read chapter two, and talk to an older Christian about it?

Have you ever stopped to think just how special you are to God? Even though we were sinners—people who didn't live for God—He chose us to be part of His family. **We didn't deserve it**, but in His loving grace He gave it to us.

You couldn't be more special to God. He sent His Son, Jesus, to die for you so you could be here today—and He planned and decided it before the world began! So when you're tempted to compare yourself to others, and you feel like you don't measure up—**remember what God has already done for you**. He made you, and He wants you to be holy and blameless in His sight. (We'll see how we do that in the rest of the book.)

7 ideas to help you

1. ***What magazines do you read?*** What's their main message? Is it that what matters most is how you look, what you can do, who you're friends with? Look through and see how many pages are like that. Ask God to help you not believe the lies.

2. ***Next time you're watching TV, look closely at the adverts.*** How many offer a product that will make your life better? How do we know these will never satisfy us? It's because the company has to keep improving the product and finding new ways to convince people. Otherwise we wouldn't keep buying it. Pray that you won't think that these products will change your life, but that you'll ask God to do that.

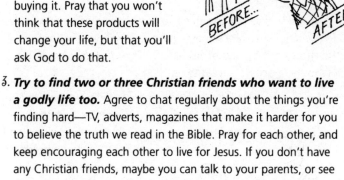

3. ***Try to find two or three Christian friends who want to live a godly life too.*** Agree to chat regularly about the things you're finding hard—TV, adverts, magazines that make it harder for you to believe the truth we read in the Bible. Pray for each other, and keep encouraging each other to live for Jesus. If you don't have any Christian friends, maybe you can talk to your parents, or see if there's a church with young people your age near by. Maybe you have friends from a camp you've been on, who you could email or phone about these things.

4. It's very easy for us only to give people compliments when they look nice or they've done something amazing. Why not think a bit differently? ***Give someone a compliment by telling them what a good friend they are***: because you can trust them so much, or they help you keep trusting Jesus, or they're kind and generous to people.

5. You probably have some younger girls who look up to you. ***Think how you can help them believe that Jesus created them exactly as He wanted them to be.*** Show them by the things you say and do that God's love for them doesn't depend on what they look like or what they do.

6. ***How long do you take getting ready in the morning?*** We can spend so much time on our hair, make-up and what to wear, that we don't have time for anything else. Read Colossians 3 v 12-14 to see what Paul tells us to be "clothed" with. Ask God to help you think about the person He has made you, and not just what you look like.

7. ***God made you who you are for a reason.*** When you get cross or upset that things aren't the way you want, try and remember to thank God for the good things in your life. Ask Him to help you trust that He knows best.

I've always worried about my looks, my weight and how others see me. My parents encouraged me to trust God but, like many teenage girls, I was self-conscious and desperate to be accepted. I hated my size. I thought if I looked a certain way, people would like me. I'd be accepted, and fit what the world says is beautiful.

Although I'd been told many times, I never fully understood what it meant to be a Christian. I thought it was about believing there is a God or going to church. I didn't understand it's actually about a personal relationship with God. I've only recently begun to see how big this is. I still have a lot more to understand.

A few months ago, I listened to a talk about faith and self-esteem. I learned that, as a Christian, my attitude towards my image should reflect God's love for me. It's God's approval that matters, and only His!

Sometimes I still worry about how the world expects me to look, and what others expect from me. What I'm trusting in affects how I think about my image. Trusting Jesus is the best thing. I don't need to rely on worldly approval. Instead I can be happy knowing that God loves me for exactly who He made me to be!

Rosie

Dive in to the Bible

Think

Is there something you wish you
could change about yourself, like Amy
Carmichael and her brown eyes? It may
be your appearance, your abilities or your popularity.

Psalm 139 tells us very clearly how much God knows about us and
that He loves us the way He has made us.

Read Psalm 139 v 1-12

Q: What does God know about us (see v 1-12)?
(There are at least five things. Can you find them?)

God knows all about us and He loves us. Psalm 139 tells us that
God is everywhere. He's with us when we're out with our friends,
on our own in our room, with our family, at school—everywhere!

Read Psalm 139 v 13-18

Q: When did God start knowing us (v 13)?

Q: How has He made us (v 14)?

You might never have knitted anything, but when you knit you
have to take care with each part. Choosing the right colour wool,
the correct needles and the right number of stitches. And following
the correct pattern to get the right item.

Q: If God "knit" us together, what does that tell us about who we are, and what God did?

Q: What do you hope you will be doing in the future?

Some of your dreams and ambitions may come true; some won't. But if your number one priority is to live for Jesus—to use the gifts and skills, the personality and abilities He's given you to live for Him—you will be the person He created you to be.

Q: How important do you think your life is to God (see v 13-14 and v 16)?

Before you were born, God thought about your whole life. He has great plans for you—the person you are, and the gifts He's given you.

Think

Will you listen to God's truth that you are "fearfully and wonderfully made"? And will you live for Him in everything you do?

Pray

- Thank God that He made you as you are because that's the way He wanted you to be.

- Ask Him to help you really believe this.

- Pray that you would show and model it to your friends.

2. The one true God

Your relationship with God

"Being a Christian is boring!"

"It's all about rules. You can't do this... You can't do that..."

"There are so many things you're not allowed to do as a Christian. Why do you bother?"

"I believe in God, but I need to have some fun. Maybe when I'm older, and I've done the things I want, I'll think about going to church and being a Christian."

Some of my school friends said these things to me. They thought because I was a Christian, my life was going to be dull forever. Why did they think that? Because they didn't understand what it means to have a relationship with God, the Creator of the world.

You might have heard all sorts of rules that Christians are supposed to obey:

X No swearing

X No drinking

X No sex before marriage

X No music or TV, unless it's about Jesus!

If people think that's what Christianity is all about, of course it sounds boring! If it's just a load of DOs and DON'Ts, who'd want to have anything to do with that? **Not me!**

Put like that it sounds terrible. It's like the moment you become a Christian all the fun stops and you just obey boring rules. You keep your Bible open in one hand to make sure what you're doing isn't against the rules—and if it is, you're in big trouble.

Well, the good news is that being a Christian isn't about rules. It isn't about being perfect. And it certainly isn't about being boring!

Being a Christian

Being a Christian...

O *is about being adopted into God's family* (Ephesians 1 v 3-5) and receiving "every spiritual blessing" (that means getting everything good that God has promised—some of it now and some of it in the future).

O *isn't about life becoming boring*. It's about us living the way God planned and intended right at the start, when He made His perfect world.

O *is about what Jesus has done for us*, not about what we have to do.

O *gives our life meaning and purpose* and that's exciting! We can know why we're here!

O *is about having a relationship with God*, who created the universe and everything in it, and who created us. (You can read about that in Genesis 1 and 2.)

Rebellion

The Bible tells us we've all rebelled against God, and our relationship with Him has been spoiled. The Bible calls this sin. Romans 3 v 23 says: "All have sinned and fall short of the glory of God". None of us are even close to being perfect. We're selfish and greedy and proud and unkind and… the list could go on.

Someone once told me that sin was like saying:

S hove off, God

I 'm in charge

N o to your ways

We think we know best; we think we can make the best decisions, so we tell God to shove off or get lost. We want to do things our own way; we don't want someone else telling us what to do.

Whenever I get a new phone, I'm very excited about using it. Reading the instruction book never looks fun—but pressing the buttons, playing with the touch screen and experimenting is great! I can usually make it work. I can call people, send messages, take pictures and connect to the internet.

But there's always more my phone can do. If I ignore the instructions, and think I can work it out myself, I'll miss some of the great things it can do. The person who made the phone knows everything about it. And they didn't keep the information secret—they wrote it down for me. If I ignore it, I'll miss out on some of the best bits.

Lots of people live life like that. They carry on without giving any thought to their Maker—to how or why they were created to work, and how they work the best. They say "Shove off" to God: *"I'm in charge; I know best"*. Then they're surprised or angry when things go wrong and don't work the way they want.

Rescue

The Bible tells us God wants what's best for us. He loves us so much and He wants to be in a relationship with us—but sin spoils that. So God sent His Son, Jesus, to earth to rescue us. Jesus never said: "Shove off, God". He always lived God's way. Yet He was arrested, beaten, nailed to a wooden cross and left to die. He didn't deserve it, **but He went through it for you and for me**, so that we could be forgiven.

God's punishment for sin is death. Romans 6 v 23 says: "The wages of sin is death". You earn wages when you work; so this verse says that our sin earns us death.

When Jesus died, He died in our place. He took the punishment that should have been ours, so that if we believe in Him, we can be forgiven. This was God's rescue plan. The end of Romans 6:23 says: "but the gift of God is eternal life in Christ Jesus our Lord". Jesus died in our place so we can have eternal life.

Jesus has done it! He's been punished for our sin, so we can live forever, for God.

We don't have to earn it. The wages of sin may be death, but eternal life is a gift from God.

Peanut butter

I wonder if you've ever thought about how much God loves you?

My brother is a big fan of peanut butter. I hate it! I can't stand the smell, or even being near the jar. Once, when we were young, my mum was ill in bed, and my brother wanted a sandwich. Of course he wanted a peanut butter one. I love my brother and wanted him to be happy. So really carefully, I got the peanut butter jar out of the cupboard, trying to touch it with just one finger and my thumb.

Yuck! Holding the jar, the knife and the bread at arm's length, I made him that sandwich (then very quickly washed my hands afterwards). Ugh—but loving my brother meant I wanted to do something for him, even though I found it hard!

What Jesus did on the cross makes my love for my brother look like nothing. Jesus chose to die on a cross, in our place, because He loves us so much and wants us to be part of His family. **That's amazing!**

We don't deserve God's love. We keep saying: "Shove off, God; I'm in charge; No to your ways". We keep on sinning; we wake up and do it every day. Romans 5 v 8 tells us that:

> *God demonstrates his own love for us in this: While we were still sinners, Christ died for us.*

Thankfully God didn't wait for us to be good enough; He knew that would never happen. The only way we could be friends with God was by Jesus taking the wage we'd earned—punishment and death—and giving us the gift of eternal life.

So what does that mean? If Jesus' death on the cross means that we can be forgiven, how does that change our relationship with God?

It means that we can begin to live the life God intended for us…

Living for God

Although we will still sin, we'll want to become more like Jesus, rather than saying "Shove off" to Him all the time… and this leads to holiness. That means becoming more like Jesus.

I did say that being a Christian isn't about following rules and it isn't. But there are some things that we cannot or will not do if we're living for Jesus.

If you're a massive Manchester United fan, you don't go out wearing a Man City shirt or telling people Man City are the best team in the world. You don't buy a season ticket for Man City, and celebrate every time they win a match. If you did, no one would believe you're a United supporter. You'd look much more like a City supporter.

If you're a Christian, your life should show it. Not because you "have to" follow rules; not because people will be disappointed in you if you don't; but because it pleases God. God gave His only Son to die in our place. Of course we'll want to live His way! **Living for Him brings real happiness.**

Being a Christian is being in a relationship with God. That's what counts. If you put Him first in everything you do, it will change everything in your life. It will mean you want to live for Him, because you love Him so much. This doesn't make life boring or full of rules. It means your best friend is the Creator of the universe, and He promises you life now, and with His people forever, where there'll be no more sin.

I wonder if you've discovered this relationship with God yet? Do you know Him as your Friend, Father and King? When you really get to know Him, and understand what He's done for you, you'll know that living for Him isn't about following rules. ***It's about loving Him and wanting to be more like Him.***

The rest of this book will help you see how you can grow in your relationship with Him, love Jesus more, and live for Him.

7 ideas to help you

1. ***Take time every day to praise and thank God for who He is.*** Looking around at His creation will help you with that. Or why not turn one of the psalms into a prayer of praise. You could also listen to some Christian music, such as Psalms from Sovereign Grace Music (www.sovereigngracemusic.org).

2. ***Make some time each day to read your Bible and pray to God.*** This will help you get to know Him better and live for Him. Bible-reading notes would help you with this, such as *Discover* or *Engage* from The Good Book Company (see page 127).

3. ***Take time regularly to say sorry to God*** for the things you do that stop you being like Him. Ask Him to help you change.

4. ***Try reading a Gospel*** (Mark is a good place to start). Learn about who Jesus is, why He came and what it means to follow Him. You could make a note of things that are really exciting, or questions you have, and talk to an older Christian about them.

5. ***Make sure you're going to church and youth group*** (if your church has one) regularly. Meeting with God's people and learning

together will help you love God more. If you're not part of a church at the moment, it's definitely an important thing to do. Maybe there's one in your town you could join, or maybe your school has a Christian Union or Fellowship you could be part of. Why not do some investigation?

6. **Try and find some Christian friends who want to live for Jesus too.** You could read this book together, helping and encouraging each other to keep living for Jesus.

7. **You could try explaining to a friend why you're a Christian**, and tell them what Jesus has done for you. If you're nervous, try writing it down first so that you know what to say.

What next?

Maybe you've got to the end of this chapter and thought: "I'm someone who tells God to shove off. I don't live for Him." And maybe you want and need to do something about it.

Don't forget, Christians are people who are forgiven, but not perfect. You may have prayed a prayer to become a Christian when you were younger, but know there are still areas in your life where you tell God to "shove off". If you're still sinning, it doesn't mean you're not a Christian. If your sin bothers you, and you wish you didn't do it, **that's a good sign that God is working in you**, and making you more like Him.

We need to say sorry to God regularly for telling Him to "shove off", and ask Him to help us change. You could use the prayer on page 25 to remind yourself of the commitment you've made to follow Jesus, and ask for His continued help.

A new start

But, maybe you've never said sorry to God, and you know you're not friends with Him. If you want to become a Christian, here are three steps that will help you:

A: Admit that you've done wrong.

Tell God you're sorry you've ignored Him and thought you can live better on your own. Tell Him you know you can't be good enough on your own.

B: Believe in what Jesus has done for you on the cross.

Believe what we're told in John 3 v 16: "For God so loved the world that he gave his one and only Son, that whoever believes in him shall not perish but have eternal life". Believe that you can be forgiven and, with God's help, live for Him.

C: Confirm that you want to live for Jesus.

Ask Jesus to come into your life and help you live for Him every day.

You could say this prayer:

Dear God,

Please forgive me for sinning against you, for telling you to shove off and saying no to Your ways. Thank You for sending Jesus to die in my place so that my sin is paid for and I can receive the gift of eternal life. Please help me to live with You in charge of my life, saying yes to Your ways. Please help to me to become more like You day by day.

Amen.

If you do pray this prayer, it would be a brilliant idea to tell an older Christian so that they can help you live for Jesus. If you don't have someone to tell at the moment, why not write down what you prayed and when, to remind yourself? **Keep reading this book** to help you learn about living for Jesus, and keep reading the Bible. Pray that God would help you get to know other Christians.

My parents are Christians, so they took me to church and youth group. But when I was 16, I began to wonder if being a Christian was what I wanted, or just something my family did. So I started to rebel. I thought I could be a Christian when I was older—after I'd had some fun.

At university, I went to church on Sunday—but for the rest of the week I did what I wanted. I cared more about how I looked and who I was with, than following Jesus. He just wasn't that important to me.

I was far away from a friendship with God. I wasn't happy. I was doing things that hurt myself and other people, and I felt really bad.

One summer I went on a Christian camp. As I listened to the teaching, it hit me how foolish I was being. I was looking for a meaning to my life, while all the time God was there. He'd sent His Son to die for me, and take the punishment I deserved. But I was ignoring Him.

I finally understood I was forgiven by God and committed my life to following Jesus. It's not always easy. Sometimes I'm tempted to turn away. But God is faithful in helping me to follow Him.

Gaby

Dive in to the Bible

Think

When you think about God, what do you think of? Which words describe Him?

Big?	*Forgiving?*
Powerful?	*Always there?*
Loving?	*Disappointed?*
Rule-giving?	*Distant?*
Stops you having fun?	*Understands us?*
Angry?	*Wants what's best?*

What we understand about God affects our relationship with Him.

Read Ephesians 2 v 1-3

Q: How does Paul describe people before they are Christians?

In verse 1?

In verse 2?

In verse 3?

It's not a great list, is it?! Let's be very clear what these mean...
Can you answer these three simple questions?

Q: What can dead things do?

Q: If you're following the ways of the world, who aren't you
   following?

Q: If we "gratify the cravings of our sinful nature" (please ourselves),
   who aren't we pleasing?

Before we're Christians we please ourselves and don't follow God.
We say: "Shove off, God; I'm in charge; No to your ways!"

The passage describes us as dead. We can't do anything about
it—dead things can't become alive! We can't stop sinning, and it
means that our relationship with God is messed up.

Q: What has God done for us in Jesus?

In verse 5?

In verse 6?

Why? "Because of his great love for us" (v 4). God didn't want to
leave us—helpless, living our own way and pleasing ourselves. God
knows the best way for us to live—and being dead in sin isn't it!

Becoming a Christian is God's work. God makes us alive. It's an amazing gift from Him.

Q: What is grace (v 8-9)?

Grace is when we get something that we don't earn or deserve. It's an undeserved gift.

Think

Will you accept the gift that Jesus has given you? The gift of making you "alive with Christ", and "raising you with Christ"; being forgiven now, and knowing that you will spend forever with God.

Pray

- Give thanks that God has made Christians alive when we were dead in sin.

- Pray that you would accept the free gift He offers.

- Ask God to help you serve Him in every part of your life.

3. Your true family

Your relationship with church

What words fill your head when you think of church?

Big? Cold? Fun? Boring? Weird? Exciting? Scary?

When I was eleven, my church building was big and cold. Actually, "cold" is an understatement; it was FREEZING! In summer, you needed a coat and gloves to go inside. In winter, I played my clarinet with gloves on which, let me tell you, is very tricky!

There were people of all ages, and I remember fun church events, youth activities and enjoying the main church service (sometimes). Some people made me feel very welcome and helped me to love being there. Others didn't.

One lady was like the fashion police. She had very strict ideas on what you should (and shouldn't) wear to church. One week I wore my new short skirt. *I loved it* and thought it looked great. I had new tights and shoes to go with it, and arrived at church feeling really good. As I walked through the door, she took one look and said:

"Oh Sarah, did you forget to put your skirt on today?"

Churches are made up of all sorts of people—different ages, backgrounds and nationalities. **One thing we have in common is that no one is perfect.** So it's no surprise that sometimes things are great, and sometimes they're hard work.

You may love church, or you may wish you never had to go again! Maybe you're secretly hoping this chapter will tell you church isn't important, and you can be a Christian without going to church. You're hoping I'll say that if your church is boring, you can stop going and just read the Bible at home instead. So let's see why I'm not going to say that…

The first church

In the book of Acts we see the very first church. Acts 2 tells us about the disciples (Jesus' twelve closest friends and followers) receiving God's Holy Spirit. They began telling people about Jesus' life, His death and that He was alive again. Jesus was back in heaven, but His followers were growing and beginning to meet together.

They [the new followers of Jesus] devoted themselves to the apostles' teaching and to the fellowship, to the breaking of bread and to prayer. Everyone was filled with awe, and many wonders and miraculous signs were done by the apostles.

All the believers were together and had everything in common. Selling their possessions and goods, they gave to anyone as he had need. Every day they continued to meet together in the temple courts. They broke bread in their homes and ate together with glad and sincere hearts, praising God and enjoying the favour of all the people. And the Lord added to their number daily those who were being saved.

Acts 2 v 42-47

They met together, ate together, looked after each other and praised God together. These first Christians "devoted themselves to the apostles' teaching"—totally committed to listening to and learning from God's Word. This gives us a good picture of what "church" should be like—Christians sharing their lives together.

Have you experienced anything like that? It's much more than spending an hour together singing and listening to a talk! If we're going to understand how important church is, we need to remember that. Even though going to church doesn't make anyone a Christian, meeting with other Christians is something we definitely need to do regularly.

Church is a family

When the Bible uses the word church, it means a group of people, not a building. *It means people of all shapes and sizes, ages and races*, who love Jesus and meet together as the family of God.

Think about your family. What do you do together? Sometimes it's probably things you all enjoy, like watch a DVD, go bowling, go for a walk, or eat pizza. There'll be some things everyone looks forward to. But I guess there are also things you have to do but don't enjoy.

My dad likes long walks—particularly walking up hills. I think hills are much nicer when you stay at the bottom and just look at them! But when I was younger, I climbed lots of hills (and mountains!) because we went as a family to do it together. I was twelve when I climbed Mount Snowdon, the highest mountain in Wales, for the first time. It was a cold, snowy day. Dad encouraged me to keep going by promising there was a shop at the top. He was right, there was a shop—but when we reached the top, it was closed. *I was not happy!*

Sometimes I enjoyed walking; sometimes I complained. But we still did it because being together as a family was important. My dad hates shopping, but sometimes he's come shopping with me even when he didn't want to. When you're part of a family, you don't just do things that please you—you think and care about others, too.

This is helpful to remember when you think about church. The people in your church are your Christian family, whether they're old, young, male, female, the same nationality as you or from somewhere else in the world. The big thing you have in common is that *you want to learn more about Jesus and grow to be more like Him.*

Sometimes we'll love being part of the church family. We'll like the songs, the talks will be great, and we'll feel like we belong. But there will be times when it's not like that. There will be songs we hate, talks that go over our heads, and people who don't understand who we are or what we want. **But that doesn't stop us being family.** If you remember that sometimes things happen the way we want and sometimes they don't, it will help you see that church is important even when you find it hard.

Imagine if every time your family decided to do something you didn't like, you refused to join in. (Maybe you do!) So each time they went out to do it, you stayed at home. Or, if they planned a family holiday, you refused to go. Or, if you had to go, you sat in the corner and sulked, looking moody and refusing to join in. Your family would be pretty miserable, wouldn't it? It wouldn't feel much like a family—not if you were acting as if you weren't part of it. In a family, everyone is important.

Our church family is the same.

Encourage each other

Hebrews 10 v 25 says:

Let us not give up meeting together, as some are in the habit of doing, but let us encourage one another—and all the more as you see the Day approaching [this means the day Jesus comes back].

If we're to "encourage one another", we need other people. It doesn't work on your own. I'd feel pretty silly going for a bike ride, and talking to myself: "Go on, Sarah, keep pedalling, you're doing a great job... I know there's a hill coming but you'll do it!" But if I'm out with a friend, and we encourage each other to keep going, it suddenly makes sense.

That's what makes church so great. I don't have to be a Christian on my own, talking to myself: "Go on Sarah, you can live as a Christian, keep believing, you're doing a great job…" I have a whole family who help me do that—older, younger, men, women, new Christians, older Christians—all encouraging me to live for Jesus. **Brilliant!**

A few years ago I'd had a really long day at work. I finally got into my car to go home, put it in reverse, and accelerated. But because I was so tired, I didn't look properly. I reversed into the brand new car of someone else in our church. Bad day!

I burst into tears, and ran out to find her. After I'd explained, she said she'd find out how much the repairs would cost—and I went home to work out how on earth I was going to pay for it, as I didn't earn much money.

The next Sunday at church someone came to me with an envelope. There was nothing written on it, and the person who gave it to me wouldn't say where it had come from. I opened it to find £300 inside—the exact amount of money to fix the car I'd hit! I went straight to find the car owner—and when I gave her the money, she gave me £30 back to mend my own car! **It was amazing.** This was my church family supporting and encouraging me, even though I'd been stupid in the first place. I felt so loved and looked after.

It's hard living for Jesus in a world where many people don't think He's important. Meeting with other Christians encourages us.

One day Jesus is coming back. We don't know when, but the day is coming. Meeting together helps us to remember that fact and make sure we're ready. The songs we sing, the talks we hear, the prayers we say, the way we love and care for each other will help us to be prepared for Jesus' return.

The writer of Hebrews doesn't say: "Meet together if you like it", or "when people understand you", or "when church is fun and exciting". He just says meet together to encourage one another.

But it's so boring...

Maybe you're thinking: "But you don't know how boring my church is!" True, but I've been to some pretty dull church services. Sometimes I wonder how people can make Jesus—the most important and exciting person in the world—sound so boring!

When I was twelve, I bought a book called *101 things to do in a dull sermon*. It had some great ideas like:

Listen for rumbling stomachs. Count how many different kinds of rumble you can hear. Time them to see which goes on for the longest.

Start from the back of the church and try to crawl all the way to the front, under the seats, without being noticed.

I never actually did any of them, but sometimes wanted to!

Now I wonder if I had the wrong attitude. I thought everything should be fun and exciting; everything should keep me happy and be exactly what I wanted to listen to. I forgot that church is made up of all different types of people. ***It's not all about me!***

Do you sometimes go to church expecting it to be dull? You don't even give it a chance. You expect to be bored, and are just waiting until you can go home and get on with the rest of your day. You don't get involved. You only talk to your friends and look miserable! Is that you?

Paul wrote to the Christians in Corinth, in southern Greece. They weren't enjoying being a church family. They thought much more about themselves than about each other. Paul told them that each of them *is like a part of the body*. (You can read it for yourself in 1 Corinthians 12 v 12-20.) He reminded them that in a body every part is important. There isn't one part that's more important than another.

If I had a head but no feet, I might decide it would be nice to go to the beach and paddle or wade. My head could think it—but without feet, paddling is going to be quite a problem! Heads are important, but they're useless on their own. In the same way that every part of the body matters, so every member of the church family is important. We all have gifts we can use to help and encourage each other. It's important that we help and look after each other.

One of the things I enjoyed most about church when I was younger was being involved and getting to know different people. I was encouraged to help with the children's work, play an instrument, do Bible readings, help with drinks—lots of different things. I got to know people, and I knew that me being there was important. *I was made to feel part of the church family, and it was good.*

Have you thought how you could get involved and serve your church family? If you're not asked to help, volunteer anyway!

Your church might have a great youth group: the teaching is good, it's fun, you meet your friends and you do things you enjoy. That's brilliant. Youth groups are really important, and we can have a great time. But youth groups aren't church. Your youth group is one part of the church family. Spending time with your youth group and your friends is important—but being part of the bigger church is crucial!

If you have a big family, you don't just talk to your brother or sister; you also spend time with your parents, aunts, uncles, grandmas and grandpas. So let's make sure we do the same in church as well. We can learn from them! It won't always be easy. We won't always understand everything or love it. But families need to meet together and encourage each other.

How could you encourage people in your church family?

7 ideas to help you

1. **Smile at people when you walk into church.** You could also try to say hello to someone you don't know, or someone who's a different age from you.

2. **Don't be afraid to ask questions.** If something happens in a church service that you don't understand, find out why it happens and why it's important.

3. At the end of a talk in church **try and write down one thing that's helped you or made you think**, and one thing that you're going to do as a result. Some churches have space on a service sheet for this, but you might prefer to get a notebook

where you could keep all these notes together. (You could write down questions you have too, and ask an older member of the church to help you understand.)

4. ***Make sure you open your Bible when it's being read***, and being taught. This will help you to listen, and will mean you can check what's being said. It will also help you remember it so you can read it again later.

5. Ask your parents or youth leaders ***how you can serve or help out in church***. What could you do to encourage your church family?

   O Maybe you can help with PowerPoint in a family service.

   O If you play an instrument, could you play in a service?

   O Can you help welcome people, or take the collection?

   O Maybe you could help serve drinks or clear away after the service.

6. ***Think about those who are younger than you.*** Your attitude towards church could be something they copy. How can you show them that meeting together as church (God's family) is important and fun? Could you offer to help with a kids' club?

7. Ask your youth leaders and your main church leaders ***how you can pray for them***.

True story: Charlotte

When I was seven, my best friend from school invited me to a church holiday club. I enjoyed it and afterwards I kept going to church with her. At first I went mostly to see my friends, but after a while I began learning more about God.

The leaders of the children's group and my friends helped teach me about a God I could know. They taught me about Jesus dying on the cross for my sin.

My friends and my church helped me get to know Jesus. Today, now I'm older, they still do. I've enjoyed getting more involved at my church. Helping with children's groups, serving as a junior leader and then main leader at Holiday Club, or even just handing out refreshments. It's helped me to feel more part of the church family. And that helps me grow in my relationship with Jesus.

Charlotte

Dive in to the Bible

Think

Think about the church you go to. Write down some words you would use to describe it—not the building, but the people and what happens.

(If you don't go to church, write down any ideas you have about what church is like.)

Read Acts 2 v 42-47

Q: What did the people in the first church "devote themselves" to (v 42)?

1:

2:

3:

4:

There are four things mentioned in verse 42:

O learning together

O meeting together

O remembering Jesus together

O praying together

Q: Do you think they're still important today? Why?

Q: How often did the Christians meet together? How much do you think they enjoyed being together (v 44-47)?

Q: Do you think other people wanted to join them and find out what they were doing? How do we know that this happened (v 47)?

The church grew. This was about 2000 years ago, and today there are churches all around the world, in many different countries—meeting to learn together, remember Jesus together and pray together.

Q: Look back at the list you made earlier. How does it compare with the first church?

Think

How can you treat your church more like a family, and make the most of being together with them?

Pray

- Give thanks for Christian believers meeting together all over the world.

- Ask God to help you grow to love your church family, and get involved.

- Pray for the other members of your church family. Ask God to help you work together as a family. Make sure you pray for specific people in your church.

4. True friendship

Your relationships with your friends

When I was thirteen, I had very long hair and often wore it loose. This was pretty annoying for anyone sitting next to me in class. We shared tables, so if I put my head on my arm as I worked, my hair spread over everything. I don't know if you've ever tried, but it's difficult writing up a science experiment with what seems like a hairy yak covering your desk!

One day I was sitting next to my best friend Sarah (not the one with beautiful feet—I went to school with lots of Sarahs!). As I lay my head on the desk and got on with my work, Sarah was getting more and more annoyed. I could hear her huffing and puffing, but I just carried on.

After a while, everyone on the table started to laugh. I looked up to see what was going on, but no one would say a word. Then Sarah held up a pair of scissors in one hand and a clump of hair in the other. **My hair!** She'd got so annoyed she'd chopped some off. Now to be honest, I had so much hair you could hardly tell—but that wasn't the point. I was furious. She found it hilarious! It took three or four days for us to talk to each other again.

Girls can be like that, can't we? Something annoys or upsets us and, instead of trying to sort it out, we stop talking to each other. It certainly wasn't the last argument I had with Sarah.

Maybe for you, the problem isn't so much trouble with your friends, but making them in the first place. You see other people make friends and have a good time, and feel like you're the only one who's left out.

Friendship matters

Friends are really important. When Jesus came to earth as a perfect man, He didn't just do things on His own. He had twelve special friends who He spent a lot of time with (Mark 3 v 13-19). And from those twelve, he had three closer friends—Peter, James and John. Jesus knew the importance of friendship—spending time and sharing lives together.

God created us to need other people. We need to be cared for and to care for others. That doesn't mean everyone can be the most popular girl in the class, or that you need lots of friends. Neither does it mean you must have a particular best friend who sticks with you through thick and thin. But we do need friends. We need people to share our lives with and to help us, as we help them.

Sadly our world is very selfish. Some people think they can manage on their own. **Many people only look out for themselves.** We see that in soap operas, reality TV shows, celebrity news and probably from our own friendships too.

People often make others look small to make themselves look big. I wonder if you've ever done that? It's very easy to do: a quick comment about how someone looks or what they've done, and a look between you and your other friends, and you can put someone else down to make yourself feel better. But remember from chapter 1—**God has created us in the very best way**. He doesn't judge us according to what we look like, or who we're friends with, so we need to be careful about how we judge others.

Christian friendship

If you're a Christian, and want to be a good Christian friend, then asking God to help you become more like Jesus is a good place to start. Jesus said:

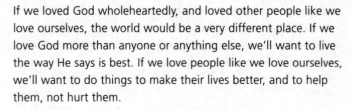

Love the Lord your God with all your heart and with all your soul and with all your mind and with all your strength.

Love your neighbour as yourself.

Mark 12 v 30-31

If we loved God wholeheartedly, and loved other people like we love ourselves, the world would be a very different place. If we love God more than anyone or anything else, we'll want to live the way He says is best. If we love people like we love ourselves, we'll want to do things to make their lives better, and to help them, not hurt them.

If you're a Christian, you've been forgiven by God—and that should change how you live. Think about the things that spoil and ruin friendships:

O jealousy   O unkind words

O greed   O spreading rumours

O selfishness   O telling lies

O anger

I bet you can think of times you've done some of these and when people have done them to you. When I look at a list like that, I'm not proud of the times I've talked about my friends behind their backs, or been jealous when a friend's better at something than me, or lost my temper and said unkind things. When Sarah cut my hair, I was pretty quick to get angry and tell others how unkind she had been, even though I was hardly the "perfect" friend.

The Bible says we need to do more than just realise that these things spoil friendships. In the book of Colossians we're told:

Put to death, therefore, whatever belongs to your earthly nature: sexual immorality, impurity, lust, evil desires and greed, which is idolatry. Because of these, the wrath of God is coming. You used to walk in these ways, in the life you once lived.

But now you must rid yourselves of all such things as these: anger, rage, malice, slander, and filthy language from your lips. Do not lie to each other, since you have taken off your old self with its practices and have put on the new self, which is being renewed in knowledge in the image of its Creator.

Colossians 3 v 5-10

Did you notice the list of things that we're to "put to death"—**to get rid of completely?** It tells us some of the things that ruin our friendships with people, and spoil our relationship with God. Paul, the writer of Colossians, says before you were a Christian you did these things, but now you're different. You have a "new self", and this new self is making you more like Jesus, the Creator.

If you've become a Christian, that list of horrible things doesn't belong to your new life. God has taken away your sin.

The death and resurrection of Jesus mean that God has forgiven you for all the wrong things you've done, and made you a new person. Paul tells us to get rid of the old life and live a new life! Keep throwing sin out of your new life. **Live the life you've been made to live.**

New clothes

Imagine a friendship without those horrible things ruining it. It would be brilliant, wouldn't it? But Paul doesn't just give us a list of "don'ts". He tells us what Jesus **helps us to do** instead. Paul tells us what our new life in Christ will look like. Instead of listing those things that ruin and spoil, in the next few verses of Colossians he writes:

> *Therefore, as God's chosen people, holy and dearly loved, clothe yourselves with compassion, kindness, humility, gentleness and patience. Bear with each other and forgive whatever grievances you may have against one another. Forgive as the Lord forgave you. And over all these virtues put on love, which binds them all together in perfect unity.*

> *Colossians 3 v 12-14*

Paul tells us to put on new clothes. **We have a whole new wardrobe.** Our old clothes (our old ways) don't fit us any more.

With Jesus' help we can put on the new clothes He's given us—
ones that show what He has done for us.

A little while ago I went cycling with a friend. It was a bright, sunny
day, but cold. We decided to ride down the towpath of the canal.
In the morning it was lovely—the sun shone, the birds sang and we
pedalled along the towpath to find somewhere to have lunch. As
we cycled, we chatted about the day, what we could see, and how
careful you need to be when you ride next to water.

Then on the way home—even after talking about it—my friend
cycled off the towpath *and into the canal*. There she was,
standing waist high in water, with her bike at the bottom of the
canal. Trying to be a good friend, I helped her and her bike out of
the water—before bursting into laughter!

When we'd both stopped laughing, she put on a dry top and we
quickly cycled home. Once she was home, my friend had a shower
and put on some warm, clean, dry clothes. It would have been
crazy if, after her shower, she'd put the wet, smelly canal clothes
back on. Her shower would have been pointless!

If Jesus has forgiven you, you've been washed clean. You
won't want to put the horrible clothes back on (greed, anger,

lies etc). You'll want to put on new clothes. You'll want to clothe yourself with all the new things Jesus has given you.

Helping your friends live for Jesus

Good friendships are brilliant; they can really help us live for Jesus. I've had Christian friends who didn't live near me, so we used to write letters to each other. We wrote two or three times a month, sharing news and encouraging each other. Sometimes we'd send Bible verses, or talk about things we'd done in our church.

I still have all the old letters—they're great to read through! Sometimes we'd phone or visit each other. If you've made some good friends on a camp or Christian holiday, keep in touch with them. It's a great way of developing Christian friendships.

Maybe, you have good Christian friends who live near you. That's great too. **Think how you can encourage each other.** My friends and I used to go to church and youth group together, which was brilliant because we could talk about it afterwards. As I've got older, I've tried to make more time to pray with my friends, and talk with them about what I've learned. They can be good at challenging me if I'm doing something that isn't helping me live for Jesus. When I'm feeling down, they remind me of how much Jesus loves me. And they celebrate with me when something exciting happens.

Imagine if every day when you left for school, as well as getting dressed, doing your hair and packing your bag, you also dressed yourself as a Christian—as the person you are. Imagine if each morning you thanked God for forgiving your sin and asked God to help you be the caring, humble, kind, gentle and patient person He's making you. Imagine if you prayed that you'd be willing to forgive people when they hurt you, and be able to love people at school, even the ones you find unlovable. Think about how it would change not only your friendships, but also the way you treat people you don't like so much.

What new clothes will you be wearing today?

7 ideas to help you

1. ***Thank God for your friends, and pray for them.*** Ask God to help you support and encourage each other even when it's tough. If you have some Christian friends, you could meet to pray together as well.

2. If you don't have many friends, and feel lonely, ***ask God to help you clothe yourself in your "Christian clothes"***. It may be best not to try and join a big group of friends, but look for one person to start with. Smile, take an interest in them, and show them you have the qualities of a good friend. If your church doesn't have any/many people your age, maybe you could ask a parent or leader if there's another church nearby with young people. Perhaps you could join up with them sometimes to meet some more people.

3. ***Type or write out Colossians 3 v 12-14*** and stick it on your mirror, or in a place where you'll see it every day, to help remind you of who you are and how God wants you to live.

4. ***Be wise about what you say.*** If you're clothing yourself in compassion, kindness, humility, gentleness and patience, this will definitely affect what you say. Don't talk about your friends

behind their backs; don't pass on secrets that aren't yours; look for ways to do the best for your friends. Why not make a decision to say something really encouraging and supportive to your friends every time you see them or email them?

5. ***Encourage your friends by trying this activity:***

   O Everyone has a piece of paper and puts their name at the top.

   O You pass the paper around the circle. On each piece of paper you see whose name it is and you write something that you admire or like about them, or something you love about your friendship. You could also add an encouraging Bible verse.

   O When your paper gets back to you, you'll be encouraged, and you'll have encouraged your friends too.

6. Look out for people at school or church or other places you go who seem to be on their own a lot. ***How could you show them love?*** How could you include them? Be patient. Sometimes people have been treated badly by friends in the past and may take time to trust you or open up to you.

7. ***Is there a friend who has hurt you in the past?*** As Christians, Jesus says we're to forgive them. This isn't always easy, but ask God to help you make the first move and try and rebuild the friendship you had. Maybe you need to say sorry to a friend you've hurt in the past. Saying sorry can be very powerful, and can be a great chance to talk about how you're trying to live for Jesus.

My dad's a minister, so talking about Jesus was normal in our house. At secondary school, I realised for the first time not everyone was a Christian. People at school thought Christians were losers. I wanted to be popular, not a loser—so I'd be a Christian on Sunday but pretend I didn't know Jesus at school.

When I was fourteen we moved from Manchester to London. I hated that and thought my mum and dad had ruined my life. I shouted at God and my parents—a lot!

That summer I went on a Christian camp. I'd heard everything they said about Jesus before, but finally it began to make sense. Jesus died to forgive me, and I needed to change my whole life, not just Sundays. Following Jesus didn't make me a loser, and I needed to show my friends I was a Christian.

Going to a new school in London made it easier to start again. From the beginning I told people I was a Christian. I made good friends at church who helped and encouraged me to live for Jesus every day.

Rachel

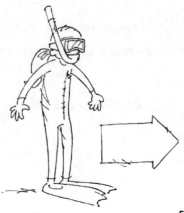

Dive in to the Bible

Think

What are the top three qualities you'd like in a friend?

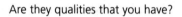

1:

2:

3:

Are they qualities that you have?

Q: How are Christians described in Colossians 3 v 12?

A new girl arrives at school. She doesn't look like the sort of person who will fit in with your group. What do you do?

a) Start chatting about her behind her back.

b) Try to include her, and make her feel welcome—but later on you and your friends discuss things you don't like about her.

c) Make an effort to get to know her. Recognise the differences but still try and include her to help her feel welcome.

Q: What answer will "God's chosen people" give?

God's chosen people won't... (see v 8)

God's chosen people will... (see v 12)

One of your Christian friends is drifting away from God and doing things that are unwise or unhelpful. What do you do?

a) Nothing—it's up to her how she lives her life.

b) Gang up on her, tell her she's a fool and she needs to change or you won't carry on being friends.

c) Talk together as a group of friends to try and work out how you can best help her. Choose one of you to go and talk to her, ask her what's going on and see how you can help out.

Q: What answer will "God's chosen people" give?

God's chosen people know that they used to... (see v 7-8)

But now they will... (see v 13-14)

Q: How would your friendships improve if you lived as verses 12-14 tell us God's chosen people should?

Think

With God's help, is there something that you need to "put to death"? How can you be a really good friend to the people you meet?

Pray

O Give thanks that God helps you get rid of the things that spoil friendships.

O Ask Him to help you to "get dressed" as you should every day.

5. Home truths

Your relationship with your parents

It was a cold, wet morning, and I was late getting up. As I rushed around, I knew if I wasn't quick, I'd be really late for school. I grabbed a piece of toast with one hand, and tried to stuff my books into my school bag with the other.

Just then, my dad walked into the room. "I've got to go out," he said. "I can drop you off at school on the way, and then you won't be late."

"Brilliant," I thought. He picked up his keys and we headed for the door.

Then I remembered what happened the last time he took me to school. EVERYONE had seen him drop me off. That should have been OK—some of my friends were brought by their parents. My problem was **I was being dropped off in a bright orange motor caravan**. You could see it (and hear it!) coming from miles off.

Loads of people had made fun of me last time. So as we arrived, I asked my dad to drop me off round the corner, where no one could see us. I thanked him for the ride and ran down the road to school, wishing again that my dad would, for once, buy a normal car like everyone else. **Why did he have to be so embarrassing?**

I wonder if you've ever felt like that? The embarrassment as you realise your parents are different from everyone else's. Or there's something your family does that you thought everyone did, but it turns out it's a "family tradition"—and quite frankly it's so embarrassing you could curl up and never leave the house again!

You may come from a family where you live with both your mum and dad. Maybe you live with just one of them, and see the other at weekends or during holidays. Maybe it's always just you and your mum, or you and your dad. Maybe you have step-parents, or you live with grandparents, or foster parents. **Families are all different.** You may find your home life easy; you may find it hard. Whatever it's like, the Bible has some teaching about living with and loving our parents, or whoever the people are who care for us and look after us day by day.

Living with parents

Parents!! They can be brilliant one minute, annoying the next, then embarrassing and then back to being brilliant! It can be hard to work out how we feel about them.

Children, obey your parents in the Lord, for this is right. "Honour your father and mother"—which is the first commandment with a promise—"that it may go well with you and that you may enjoy long life on the earth."

Ephesians 6 v 1-3

Paul, who wrote the letter to the Ephesians, says children should obey their parents. Hold on a minute! Obey our parents? Surely he can't mean all the time! He must know that parents sometimes make stupid rules, or are just plain annoying!

What about rules like:

O **No TV until homework is done.** (Everyone knows you need a break after school before you have to do more work!)

O **If you've been off school, then you can't go out in the evening.** (But what if a day off school means you're feeling well enough to go out in the evening?)

What about when parents make up rules, or stop you doing things they do themselves? How annoying is that? Surely if our parents are unfair, ridiculous or downright mean, you don't have to obey them.

Obey your parents in the Lord...

We often think we know better than our parents, don't we? What do they know? They're "so old", "so boring", "always want to spoil our fun"… But the Bible tells us clearly that we should "obey our parents in the Lord, for this is right". God tells us we should obey our parents. But why?

Obey your parents in the Lord...

This may seem like a weird phrase. Earlier in this book (chapters 2 and 4) we said that if Jesus has forgiven you, you'll want to live a life that shows it, a life that pleases God. "Obey your parents in the Lord" means obey your parents because you love Jesus and have been forgiven by Him. (That doesn't mean if you're not a Christian, you won't love your parents—but loving Jesus affects how you love other people.) **Loving Jesus changes the way that you love and obey your parents.**

O If you love Jesus, you'll want to follow His way.

O If you love Jesus, you'll know that obeying your parents shows that you're obeying and honouring God.

How you treat your parents (or the adults who look after you), how you listen to and obey them, will show whether you're really loving and obeying God. If every time they ask you to do something—like tidy up, look after your sister, come to a meal on time or go to church with them—you whine and complain and make a fuss, what does that tell you?

Are you showing that you're following Jesus, and following His ways?

Are you obeying your parents in the Lord?

...For this is right

Obey your parents in the Lord, for this is right.

The Bible says it is right for us to obey parents. That means God says it is right. He made us and knows what we need. When animals are born, most of them can soon walk, find food, feed themselves and sometimes live on their own. Last year I saw a calf being born. It was amazing. Within moments he was taking his first few steps in the field. Humans are very different: we can't look after ourselves after a few days, a few weeks or even a few years! (Even though I'm an adult, I still phone my mum and dad with all sorts of questions.)

We need adults to care for us and look after us. God created families to do just that. It's the job of mums and dads to love and care for us, guide us, help us and discipline us when we need it. Sadly, not all families work in the best way, and not all families are the way we might like. But God knows that children need to be looked after, not just with food, clothes and shelter but with love and care, and teaching about Him too.

I was finally allowed a TV in my bedroom when I was 13. It was very exciting. Many of my friends had had one for ages. I felt like I was years behind them. Now believe it or not, a few years ago televisions didn't all come with a remote control. My TV was like that. One night as I went to bed, there was a film I wanted to watch, but my mum said no. There were probably two reasons for this:

1. It was late and I had school the next day.

2. The film wasn't a good one for me to watch.

So I went to bed and switched off the TV. When my mum had been in to say goodnight, I switched it back on again. I decided it was ok; she'd never know! But to hide the fact that I was disobeying her, I had to turn the sound right down. And because there was no remote control, I had to stand in front of the TV to do it. In fact I spent nearly an hour 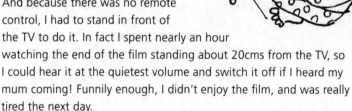 watching the end of the film standing about 20cms from the TV, so I could hear it at the quietest volume and switch it off if I heard my mum coming! Funnily enough, I didn't enjoy the film, and was really tired the next day.

I thought my mum was unfair and spoiling my fun. I thought I knew best, when actually she knew best. She wanted to protect me from watching things that weren't good for me, and help me be ready for school the next day.

God's way is best

God decided that children should have parents to care for them and have authority over them, because it was the best way. We should obey our parents because it is right. God created families for our good—to help us grow!

Ephesians 6 v 2-3 says:

> *"Honour your father and mother ... that it may go well with you and that you may enjoy long life on the earth."*

God says that obeying our parents will affect how we enjoy life. Authority is often seen as a bad thing. No one really likes having someone else telling them what to do. **But it's really important.**

Imagine you need to have your tonsils taken out. You're sitting in the hospital when a newly qualified doctor comes in. He smiles at you and says: " I've come up with a new way to take tonsils out. I don't think the doctors who taught me know the best way, so we're going to do it my way." What if that turned out to be doing the operation on your dining-room table without any anaesthetic or painkillers? That wouldn't be good. I'm sure you'd prefer your new doctor to listen and learn from older and wiser doctors. Otherwise it would have serious consequences—like a lot of pain and screaming!

Listening to the wisdom and experience of our parents, and respecting their authority, is really important and will have consequences for us and for others. A world where everyone thinks they know best, and makes their own decisions without listening to anyone older and wiser, would be a mess. **God's way is best.**

Maybe your mum and/or dad are Christians. Although you make mistakes, and so do your parents, you know they're trying to help you become more like Jesus. If you do have Christian parents, that's a real privilege. You should remember to thank God for them, and pray for them regularly that they will keep following Jesus, and help you to do the same.

But maybe you're a Christian, and one or both of your parents don't follow Jesus. **That doesn't mean you can ignore this verse in the Bible.** Children are taught to obey their parents in the Lord, for this is right! As you love and obey them, you can show them that loving Jesus changes how you live. If you're trying to follow Jesus, but your parents aren't, you can show them by the way you live that Jesus is so important that following Him affects everything—even the way you talk to them and obey their rules, however crazy they may seem!

A few years ago I knew a girl who became a Christian after going to a lunchtime Christian group at school. She started coming along to church and midweek youth group and was growing as a Christian. When she was about 14, her mum, who wasn't a Christian, told her she couldn't go to church anymore. The girl and I talked about what she should do. After looking at the Bible, we agreed that she should obey her mum. Although going to church is important, she could continue to read her Bible at home and she could go to lunchtime group at school—there were other places where she could meet with God's people and learn from His Word.

As she obeyed her mum, she showed her mum that following Jesus really mattered to her, and obeying His Word (and her mum's) was also important. After a while, her mum changed her mind, and allowed her to come to church again. She saw that following Jesus was important to her daughter.

Will you obey your parents? Will you obey God's words and trust that He knows best?

7 ideas to help you

1. **Pray for your parents**, or whoever looks after you, and thank God for them. If they're Christians, pray that they will keep following Jesus and help you to do the same. If they're not Christians, pray that you will show them by the way you live how important Jesus is, and that God will bring them to know Him too.

2. Sometimes we obey our parents, yet make it very clear we don't really want to or don't agree with them. **Ask God to help you to obey them cheerfully.** If you disagree with them, try talking to them about it rather than shouting or sulking or doing your own thing anyway.

3. **Talk to your parents.** Ask them about what they've been doing, and tell them about what you've been doing. Plan to keep spending time together. My mum and I used to watch period dramas together (things like *Pride and Prejudice* and *Emma*) because we both enjoyed it!

4. It can be a tough job being a parent, so **ask about things you can do to help them**. You may be able to help around the house, with your brothers and sisters, or in other ways.

5. If your mum or dad is a Christian, **ask them when they became a Christian** and how they get to know God better and keep living for Him.

6. Maybe you have a difficult relationship with one or both of your parents. It might be helpful to **talk to a youth leader or older Christian** about this. Extra adults in our lives are very helpful, but they don't replace our parents (or those who care for us day by day).

7. Everyone's home life is different. If you know someone whose family life isn't that easy, **pray about how you can be a good friend to them** and support them. You could also pray for children around the world growing up without parents or people to love and care for them.

I became a Christian on a summer camp. On the way home I was excited to start living with Jesus as my King—but also slightly scared about how my parents would react to this change in my life. I've been fortunate that my parents have never stopped me going back to camp or going to church. (My dad has regularly driven me on a Sunday evening!) I've never felt torn between obeying my parents and obeying God because they've been very supportive.

Although this is great, they've never shown an interest in wanting to know Jesus themselves. I still feel nervous at the thought of talking to them about Jesus. I pray that my actions show what a huge difference knowing Jesus has on my life and that they will come to know Him that way.

It can be hard when I feel my parents expect me to behave in a worldly way and long for worldly things, but I get a lot of encouragement from my Christian friends. It's especially great to have friends who are in the same situation.

Lucy

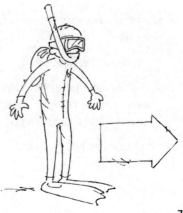

Dive in to the Bible

Think

Think of three things you love about your parents and three things you find hard.

I love…

1:

2:

3:

I find hard…

1:

2:

3:

Why are parents so important?

Read Ephesians 6 v 1

Q: Why isn't obeying your parents optional?

Sometimes we obey our parents but make it very clear we don't want to.

Think about these situations:

1: You're reading your Bible and praying one evening when your dad calls from the kitchen. "I want you to help with the drying up… now!" What should you do?

a) Say: "Sorry, I'm praying at the moment. I'll be down in 15 minutes."

b) Go down and help, moaning and grumbling about the fact that you were busy reading your Bible, and how "out of order and unfair" your dad is.

c) Go down and help in a good mood—after all, you can read your Bible when you've finished.

2: Your parents, who aren't Christians, say you can't go to church because they want you to spend time with them on a Sunday. What should you do?

a) Ignore them and go anyway. Listening to God is more important than obeying such a stupid and unfair rule.

b) Obey your parents, and maybe join a lunchtime group at school where you can meet with other Christians. Talk to your youth leader at church and look for some Christian friends to help support you.

c) Obey your parents and not go, but complain about it at every chance you get, telling them how unfair and unreasonable they are being.

Q: How does Ephesians 6 v 1-3 help you decide what to do?

Think about your relationship with those who care for you. What do you need to remember, and put into practice?

Pray

O Give thanks for your parents and the way they look after you.

O Ask God to help you be obedient.

O Pray that, even when your relationship with your parents is difficult, you'll keep living God's way.

6. True love

Your relationships with boys

One cold, sunny afternoon I was on a walk organized by church. Loads of people were there— but most importantly, Chris was there. I'd liked him for ages. My friends knew I liked him, and this walk was the perfect opportunity for us to get to know each other better. During the walk we talked about next week's dance. One of my friends said: "Hey Chris, you should dance with Sarah". He looked at me, smiled, and said: "OK then, I will!"

The week dragged as I waited for Saturday night to come. Mid-way through the evening, Chris asked me to dance. ***It was brilliant!*** We chatted lots that evening and I had an amazing time. That night I wrote all about the evening in my diary: what he wore, what he said, everything! I was getting excited and carried away about what it could mean and what could happen!

In my excitement, I forgot to hide my diary, and accidentally left it on my desk. A week later I was at youth group, when my brother and his friend started reciting "word for word" things I'd written about Chris.

They'd read and remembered my diary. **I could have died.** Thankfully Chris wasn't there. I didn't want him to hear what I'd written about him!

Nothing ever happened between us—and a few years later he went out with my best friend!

Boys—good or bad?

Boys are confusing. When we're little, we don't mind playing with them—and then overnight they suddenly become annoying! I have two brothers. They were irritating enough, but their friends were even worse. **Ugh!**

Then things change again. We want to spend time with boys and want them to notice us. They stop being annoying (well, some of them!) and start being interesting. We begin to like (or fancy) one particular boy more than others. We're excited about seeing him, more conscious about what we look like, and jealous when he spends too much time talking to other girls.

You might not feel like that about boys at the moment. You may enjoy having boys as friends, but you're not attracted to any of them. **That's fine**; everyone's different and it's nothing to worry about. This chapter will still be helpful though, as it's good to be prepared for what is likely to happen in the future.

Maybe you fancy someone and you're upset he hasn't noticed you, or maybe a boy fancies you but you don't like him. Maybe you have a boyfriend. Perhaps someone asked you out and you're not sure what to do. Maybe you're a bit confused about who you like—you like boys, but you find yourself admiring girls too and you're not really sure what's going on.

Love story

In almost every TV show, film or song there seems to be a bit of a "love story". Celebrity magazines have headlines about who's been seen with who, or who's been dumped by who. People say we live in a sex-obsessed society, which suggests that all people think about is who they fancy and how they can get together with them.

Do you ever think about the magazines and books you read, the films you watch and music you listen to? Have you thought about the message they give about boys and relationships? It's easy to watch, read and listen to things without thinking about them. But the danger is that we start to believe the big ideas put across. Like:

"You're weird if you don't have a boyfriend."

"Relationships are all about making you happy."

"Sex isn't a big deal—so just do it!"

"It doesn't matter if you love a boy or a girl—do what feels right."

It's hard to live God's way in a world where having a boyfriend is seen as more important than having a relationship with God.

O What should you do if you like a boy or a boy likes you?

o What if you're already going out with someone?

o What if you're confused about who you fancy?

This chapter won't answer every question you have but it will help you see what the Bible says about relationships and sex.

What does the Bible say?

The Bible doesn't really say anything about people going out with each other. This is because in Bible times relationships were very different. People got married much younger, and didn't really bother with the boyfriend/girlfriend stage! However, *it does tell us how we can be "pure" in our relationships*; spotless, living the way God says is best.

Paul wrote a letter to the Christians living in Thessalonica, in northern Greece. (He really did do a lot of letter writing. Think how much easier his life would have been if email had been invented!) In chapter 4 he gives them this advice:

> *It is God's will that you should be sanctified: that you should avoid sexual immorality; that each of you should learn to control your own body in a way that is holy and honourable, not in passionate lust like the pagans, who do not know God; and that in this matter no-one should wrong or take advantage of a brother or sister. The Lord will punish all those who commit such sins, as we told you and warned you before. For God did not call us to be impure, but to live a holy life.*
>
> *1 Thessalonians 4 v 3-7 (TNIV)*

There are three big things that God wants for His people:

O He wants them to avoid sexual immorality (v 3).

O He wants them to control their own body (v 4).

O He wants them to treat other people right (v 6).

Why? "It is God's will that you should be sanctified" (v 3). God wants you to be "holy" (v 7). Sanctified and holy mean set apart, pure, clean, spotless. God made you and He knows this is the best way to live.

1: Avoid sexual immorality

Some people think God hates sex. He doesn't. God created sex and says it's brilliant. He made Eve especially for Adam and told them they are to be "one flesh" (Genesis 2 v 24). They were to love each other, and one way they would show this was by having sex, and having children.

God says that the only right place for sex is in a marriage between a man and a woman—two people who love and commit to each other for life. So if we imagine sex is ok if we really love someone, or if we've been together a long time, then we're wrong! We should avoid things that don't take sex as seriously as God does.

But, we can be "sexually immoral" without having sex, so Paul has more advice for us...

2: Control your own body

One day some friends and I were discussing things we were good at. I was very confident about my gymnastic ability. "I can kick my leg higher than my head," I stated boldly. Some people were impressed, but others didn't believe me. "Watch this!" I said.

I took a few steps back and kicked. I wasn't expecting what happened next! Instead of applause, and cries of "Wow Sarah, you're amazing," everyone laughed! Why? I'd done it; I'd kicked my leg higher than my head. Sadly, as I did it, **I kneed myself in the chin!**

The look of shock and pain on my face as my leg came down made everyone roar with laughter. Having made such a great claim at the beginning, I'd then lost control of my own body! Embarrassing!

Thankfully, most of the time we can control our bodies. So why does Paul say: "Each of you should learn to control his own body in a way that is holy and honourable"? Surely it's easy? Well, it can be—but sometimes it's really hard—and the more you like a boy, the harder it can be.

God created us to be sexual people; so when you like a boy, unusual things start to happen to your body. Paul is warning us about this. Keeping control of your feelings and desires will help you to keep living God's way.

Think

It's easy to daydream about boys: imagining places you might meet, things you might do, being kissed… It's easy to lose control of your thoughts. This is dangerous.

O Would the boy be happy he's in your thoughts in this way?

O Are you doing things in your mind you definitely wouldn't and shouldn't be doing in real life?

O Do you prefer your make-believe world to your real one?

O Are your thoughts helping you to stay pure?

Control your mind! If you start thinking about boys in the wrong way, think about something else: read a book, phone a friend, ask God to help you control your mind! Change your thoughts, because these thoughts won't help you to live a holy life.

Say

Do you talk about boys a lot with your friends? Who you fancy, who you hope fancies you, what he said, what he did, what it means?

It's easy for our conversations to get out of control. Sometimes we forget God altogether and just think about what makes us happy. Conversations affect how we think! They can lead to daydreams and unhelpful thoughts.

Do

What you think and say affects what you do. So thinking about who you talk to, how you act and how you treat people is important.

Boys get excited by what they see, so how you look and behave matters.

O Are you a different person when you're around boys?

O Do you pretend you can do things you can't?

O Do you do things to get boys to notice you?

O Do you dress to impress?

Be yourself! We should treat boys as brothers (1 Timothy 5 v 1), loving them and being wise about how we act.

3: Treat other people right

We can sometimes forget that boys have feelings too. Verse 6 says:

...no one should wrong or take advantage of a brother or sister.

We can do that by flirting. For example:

You know a boy likes you, and you realise that if you dress in a tight or low-cut top, or smile a lot, he's happy to do things for you. You don't like him; you're just using him to get what you want. This is unkind and can end up seriously hurting him and you.

Sometimes we do this on purpose and sometimes because we don't think.

Sometimes we're mean to someone when he says he likes us, because we don't like him.

People are made in the image of God. That means boys too, so we must treat them right. **Friendships with boys can be great fun!** Even if you're not ready to have a boyfriend, having boys as friends is important. Boys aren't just there to be people we can fancy.

It's important to get to know boys and enjoy spending time together. Find things that you have in common; talk together and talk about Jesus. Being wise about your friendships with boys, before you think about going out or getting married, will help you when you start thinking more seriously about them.

1 Thessalonians 4 v 3-7 isn't just written for girls or for boys. These verses are a challenge to all Christians about pure and holy relationships. Avoiding sexual immorality, controlling your body and treating others right are essential.

You'll meet boys at school, church, clubs and other places, so it's important to think carefully about a boy you become close friends with.

Is he committed to…

O following Jesus with all his heart?

O avoiding sexual immorality?

O controlling his own body?

O treating other people right?

If the answer is no to any of those questions, think carefully about what that could mean for you, and your commitment to living for Jesus. ***It will make it very hard!***

In the future, you may get married or you may stay single, but being careful in your relationships now is the best way to start. It will show that you're committed to following Jesus, loving other people and loving yourself.

7 ideas to help you

1. ***Think about the conversations you and your friends have about boys*** in your class or church, or boys you see on TV. What do you talk about? Would you be happy if the boy was listening to your conversation? Are you happy Jesus is listening?

2. ***How do you act around boys?*** Do you find yourself trying to get their attention? Do you dress to get them to notice you? Do you act differently with boys than with girls? Ask God to help you treat boys right. Sometimes we do these things to make ourselves feel more attractive and to feel special. Have another look at chapter 1 to remind yourself of what God thinks about you.

3. ***Think about what you wear and what you do.*** Do your clothes, your words, and your actions help boys to "control their bodies"? If you're flirting, and wearing clothes that show off your body and reveal a lot of skin, is that going to help boys to "think pure thoughts"? Remember, we've said that what we think about affects what we do. The same is true for boys. You can treat others right by being wise about the things you say, do and wear.

4. ***Look at some of the relationships you see in films or TV shows*** and between celebrities. What words would you use to describe them? Are they trying to live God's way? If not, think about some of the consequences. How would living God's way change them?

5. Relationships with boys can be very exciting, but ***think really carefully before spending lots of your time with just one person***. It's much easier to control your own body and treat others

right when you're in a group of friends. Ask God to help you to be wise.

6. ***Do you really want a boyfriend? Think about why.*** Some people think if you haven't got a boyfriend, there's something wrong with you. Many magazines will make you feel like that. Maybe your friends do, too. Having a boyfriend doesn't make life perfect. Only a relationship with Jesus can really give us the best life. Jesus had the best relationship with God, and He never had a girlfriend or got married. Don't believe the lies, and don't agree to go out with someone just so you have a boyfriend—you'll only end up hurting him and probably yourself as well. Pray that God would help you to remember His way is best and trust Him.

7. ***Maybe reading this chapter has left you feeling confused.*** You're not really interested in boys yet; you prefer being with your girlfriends instead. That's quite normal; some girls don't become interested in boys until they're much older. However, if you think that you might like girls instead of boys, it would probably be helpful to talk with an older Christian friend who you trust. You could also look at

www.truefreedomtrust.co.uk/for_young_people

for some help and advice.

My parents are Christians, but as a teenager I wasn't bothered about knowing God. I had more important things to worry about: popularity, looks, fashion, boys, school. These things were OK, but they didn't make me happy.

My boyfriend wasn't a Christian. He was only interested in what I looked like; not helping me follow Jesus. We went out for two years and breaking up was hard, but Christian camps helped me see that the relationship wasn't helping me.

Recently I started praying God wouldn't let me have a boyfriend unless he's a Christian. Waiting is ok! Sometimes I'm lonely, especially when my friends have boyfriends, but I'm sure God knows what's happening in my life. A godly guy is the top of my list: someone to encourage me, teach me, and share my faith—someone living for Jesus.

When I loved my boyfriend more than anything, my world came crashing down when it ended. But now that I know God is the love of my life, and that He'll be the love of any future boyfriend as well, I'm secure. God's love never changes—boyfriend or not, I'm loved!

Lora

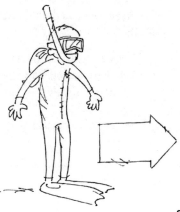

Dive in to the Bible

Read 1 Thessalonians 4 v 3-7

Q: What things make it hard for you
"control your own body in a way that is
holy and honourable" (v 4)?

Q: Many books, films, TV shows and songs
don't really care about us being "holy"
(v 7). What can help you to be holy and go
against the flow?

There's a boy at school you fancy. He's not a Christian, but you think
he likes you. He says you look nice, and he makes you feel good. You
think about him a lot! What should you do?

a) Keep spending time with him; flirt, dress to impress, and hope
he'll ask you out. Other people have boyfriends; why shouldn't
you?

b) Decide that because he's not a Christian, you need to be wise
about how you act and what you wear. You want to be his
friend but you can't go out with him as it won't help you be
holy.

c) Decide that because he's not a Christian, you can't be friends
with him. So you start ignoring him, and telling people you're
no longer friends.

Q: How would 1 Thessalonians 4 v 3-6 help you decide what to do?

There's a Christian boy that you know, and you enjoy spending time together. Do you...

a) Daydream about him when you're not together, imagine you're going out (maybe getting married), and imagine conversations you could have?

b) Spend more and more time with him? You tell your other friends he's a Christian so it's ok, but you're seeing your friends less and less.

c) Spend time with him, but make sure you regularly include your other friends? Find things you all enjoy doing together, including things at church, so you're all serving and having fun together.

Q: How would 1 Timothy 5 v 1-2 help you decide what to do?

Being holy isn't something that starts when you're an adult. It's something God always wants us to be, in every relationship.

Think

Are you taking your "holiness" seriously?

Pray

O Ask God to help you be pure and holy in the way you treat boys you know.

O Ask Him to help you make good and wise decisions about who you spend time with and grow close to.

7. Truth or dare

Your relationships with non-Christians

I used to help with an after-school Christian club for children aged 5-11. It was great fun, and the kids loved it. We played games, made things, ate snacks, sang songs and learned stories from the Bible. We didn't advertise it much because the children did it themselves, especially the 5-7s. They'd go to school, and say to their friends:

"Would you like to come to our club? It's really fun. We play games and make things and learn about Jesus."

And their friends would come along. They didn't seem to find it difficult inviting people or saying their club was about Jesus. They liked the club, so wanted their friends to be there too.

Sometimes, things that are easy when we're young become a lot harder when we're older. Think how quickly you can learn how to use a new phone, and how much longer it takes your mum or your granny!

Imagine saying to one of your school friends who isn't a Christian:

"Would you like to come to church? It's really fun and we get to learn about Jesus."

Would you find it easy? If you would, that's great—keep doing it. It's brilliant to invite people to things you know will help them hear the truth of the Bible so they can come to know Jesus for themselves.

But often inviting our friends to church or youth group, or telling people about what we believe, is really hard. Maybe you know it's important, and you want to do it, but you just can't. Or perhaps you're not sure it's important—why can't everyone just believe what they want to?

The only way to God

Why do we need a whole chapter about our relationships with people who aren't Christians? If you're a Christian, you know how important Jesus is. Jesus says He is the only way to God—that no one comes to the Father except through Him (John 14 v 6). Unless we believe and trust in Jesus, and what He did on the cross to bring us forgiveness, we can't be with God. We can't be friends with Him now on earth, and we won't be friends with Him forever in eternity.

That's serious. God is good and loving. He wants people to be friends with Him forever. But if people choose to ignore and reject Him on earth, He'll let that continue forever. That's a very long time—and it won't be nice at all, living in a place without a good and loving God.

As a Christian, I don't want people to end up separated from God. I know how great it is to follow Him now and what it means for the future. I should want to pass that news on to other people. It should be something we love to do; but we often find it very hard.

When I'm at home and reading the
Bible, I truly believe what it says. I know
separation from God is terrible and I
think: "OK, I'm going to tell people about
Jesus today so that they can come to
know Him too." So I decide to phone a
friend who's not a Christian. We chat for
a while about what we've been doing
and how things are going, and then we

hang up. As I put the phone down, I realise I didn't even mention
Jesus, let alone talk about how great it is to follow Him.

I wonder if that ever happens to you. You know it's a good thing,
but you either forget, or you panic, or you think they wouldn't be
interested or will laugh at you. So, although the name Jesus may be
on the tip of your tongue all day, He never gets mentioned!

Now try to imagine being like Peter and John, two of Jesus' disciples.
When they were arrested for speaking about Jesus they said:

"We cannot help speaking about what we have seen and heard."

Acts 4 v 20

Nothing, not even the threat of prison, stopped them talking about
Jesus.

How can we talk about Jesus when many people think He's a joke or don't believe in Him, or they belong to a different religion? How can we be brave enough to talk to people about Jesus?

On our own we can't! We can't convince people and change people's minds. But God can! So the first thing we need to do is pray.

Talk to God about people

Paul wrote to the Christians living in the town of Colosse, in what is now Turkey. Paul wrote:

> *Devote yourselves to prayer, being watchful and thankful. And pray for us, too, that God may open a door for our message, so that we may proclaim the mystery of Christ, for which I am in chains.*

Colossians 4 v 2-3

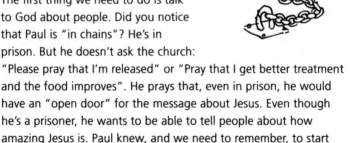

The first thing we need to do is talk to God about people. Did you notice that Paul is "in chains"? He's in prison. But he doesn't ask the church: "Please pray that I'm released" or "Pray that I get better treatment and the food improves". He prays that, even in prison, he would have an "open door" for the message about Jesus. Even though he's a prisoner, he wants to be able to tell people about how amazing Jesus is. Paul knew, and we need to remember, to start with prayer.

"Devote yourselves to prayer, being watchful and thankful." **Start with prayer**, talking to God about people. If we do, it will help us remember that we can't change people's hearts and minds. We can't make anyone understand and believe in Jesus—only God can do that. **So pray.**

We can pray for people we know who aren't Christians, and pray for them by name. "Father God, I want to pray for my friend, Sally…" We can pray that they will want to hear the truth, will be ready to listen, and will understand. We can also pray that God will "open doors"—that He will give us opportunities to talk to people about Jesus.

Talk to people about God

When we've prayed for people, and asked God to give us opportunities, we need to talk to people about God. That's the next part of Paul's letter:

Pray that I may proclaim it [the good news about Jesus] clearly, as I should. Be wise in the way you act toward outsiders; make the most of every opportunity. Let your conversation be always full of grace, seasoned with salt, so that you may know how to answer everyone.

Colossians 4 v 4-6

Paul asks the church to pray that he would "proclaim" the good news; that he would talk about Jesus. He wants his readers to do the same. If you've prayed to God about someone you'd like to talk to, don't be surprised when God gives you an opportunity to do just that!

So if you ask God to help you talk to your friend about Jesus, and on Monday morning she says to you: "What did you do yesterday?"—tell her what you learned in church. If someone asks you if you've read any good books lately, or seen any good websites, or heard any good new songs—tell them about a Christian book, website or band you know about. Tell them something exciting you've read in the Bible.

If you pray that God will open doors, **He will open them**. He'll help you to walk through them; He'll help you to talk about Him. With God's help you can begin conversations about Him. It's scary at first, but it becomes easier with practice. And God will be helping you every step of the way.

A few weeks ago my neighbour, who I hadn't met before, got locked out of her house. I invited her in to keep warm and wait for someone with a key. As we sat drinking tea, she asked what my job was. I told her I'm a church youth worker. Then she asked why I wanted to be a youth worker. It was definitely an opening to tell her about what I believed, and why I thought teaching young people about Jesus was so important. God gave me an opportunity: **He opened a door, and I tried to use it as best I could**.

Paul says we need to think about what we do and what we say:

> *Be wise in the way you act toward outsiders; make the most of every opportunity.*
>
> *Colossians 4 v 5*

We should:

- O talk about Jesus
- O talk like Jesus
- O talk because of Jesus

1: Talk about Jesus

Very few films, TV shows or books even mention Jesus, so it's easy for people to think He's not that important. But if we talk about Jesus with our friends regularly, we can help them see He's important to us. We can tell them about things we've learned at church, or from reading the Bible.

It would be weird to have a best friend and never mention them when you're with your other friends—so we should make it normal to talk about our best friend, Jesus.

2: Talk like Jesus

When I was at school, I tried hard not to swear because I know as a Christian what I say is important. Many people at school swore without thinking and it would have been easy to go along with them. Sometimes my friends did their best to get me to swear and I tried really hard not to join in.

Unfortunately there were times when I failed, and got so cross that I swore. The news would spread like wildfire: "You'll never guess what Sarah said…". It didn't happen very often, so it was a shock.

I wish I could say the same about gossip and talking behind people's backs. Again, I tried, but it was really hard. There were definitely too many times when I found myself saying things like: "Guess what Sabeena said…" or "Have you heard about Emma and Dave…?" I wasn't being wise in the way I acted, or showing people that I was a Christian all day every day.

Jesus didn't use words to hurt people, or to be rude to people. If we want to show people that Jesus is important, we must use our words like Jesus did.

Do you live and speak a life that shows Jesus? At home, at school, when you're out with your friends? If the way you act and speak is no different to everyone else, why would they bother thinking about becoming a Christian? They'll think it makes no difference to life. If your friends know you're a Christian—**live like one**.

3: Talk because of Jesus

Talking *about* Jesus and *like* Him is brilliant! But we also need to talk *because* of Him. That means telling people that the death and resurrection of Jesus means we can be forgiven. If we've been forgiven, we want other people to know that forgiveness too.

Let your conversation be always full of grace, seasoned with salt, so that you may know how to answer everyone.

Colossians 4 v 6

"Full of grace"—means being loving and gentle in all I say. If I'm talking with grace, I won't just walk up to a friend out of the blue and say: "Hey Abigail, if you don't believe in Jesus, you're going to hell". She won't listen to me. It's not loving and gentle. It would be more loving to talk regularly about Jesus, and show how important Jesus is in my everyday life.

But there are some hard truths in the Bible, and Paul also says our conversation should be "seasoned with salt". That means being interesting and wise, but also being willing to say things that are true even though it's hard. If someone asks: "Do you believe Jesus is the only way to God?", the answer must be yes, because the Bible says so. We shouldn't try to give an answer that will keep everyone happy—we must tell people what the Bible actually says.

Sometimes our conversations about Jesus will be with our friends; sometimes we might be in a class or in a big group. Whoever we're with, we need to speak with grace, not thinking we're better than others or getting angry. We're not trying to "make" people Christians by having the loudest voice or the most convincing argument. We want people to understand how brilliant Jesus is.

Sometimes I had good conversations with friends; other times I felt tongue-tied and didn't know what to say. I was worried they'd laugh or ask a question I couldn't answer. So I invited friends to come to church or youth group with me. That way they heard other people talking about Jesus too, and I had help to answer their questions and explain what I believed. You could do that, and then talk to your friend about it afterwards.

It can be scary—we worry about what people will think, say and do—but God is with us and He loves us to tell people about Him. Even if things don't go well, and people aren't interested, **God is with us every step of the way**. We can keep talking to Him and knowing He's with us.

I've had some good and some bad experiences. Sometimes people have laughed at me because they think I'm crazy. At times they've told me very strongly that they're not interested. But sometimes friends have come to events, or had conversations with me. I keep praying that those who still don't know Jesus will come to know and love Him for themselves. That would be brilliant!

7 ideas to help you

1. **Think of the names of two or three people who you know aren't Christians.** Write them on a piece of paper and put them in your Bible. Why not commit to praying for them every day, asking that they will come to know Jesus? Ask God to give you opportunities to talk to them, and that they'd ask questions.

2. **No one likes a lecture. So think about what you say.** Maybe tell your friend one thing like "We had a great time looking at the Bible in youth group yesterday" or "I read an amazing chapter in the Bible last night" and stop. If they ask you a question, tell them a little bit more. Beforehand (and during, in your head!) you can pray that your friend will be interested—but let them ask to find out more if they want to.

3. **If you have a Christian group at your school, get involved.** That could be a brilliant place to take someone if they start to show an interest. (If there isn't a Christian group, could you help get one started? Talk to some other Christians in school if you know any, and try to find a Christian teacher.)

4. **Talk to your youth leader, if you have one, about the people you're praying for.** There may be an event at youth group or church that would be particularly good to invite your friends to. Pray for them with that in mind.

5. **Don't be discouraged if your friends aren't interested.** It's not your fault. One boy I know was a bit down one day. His leader asked him why, and he replied: "We're having a guest service and I don't think I should come. I've invited ten of my friends and they all said no." Although it was sad that his friends couldn't or wouldn't come, the fact that he had invited them was brilliant. So talk to people—but don't blame yourself if they say no.

6. **Why not learn a quick and simple way of explaining the good news about Jesus?** There are some suggestions on page 126. Then if someone asks you, "What is a Christian?" or "What is it that you believe anyway?" you can be confident you know what to say.

7. **Don't feel you have to answer every question you're asked.** If a friend asks questions you can't answer, admit you don't know the answer and suggest that together you talk to an older Christian you trust. Or tell your friend you'll ask someone and get back to them. It's better to make them wait than give a crazy answer.

I don't remember thinking about God when I was little. My family didn't mention Him and I didn't know who Jesus was. I remember going to church with my grandma when I was seven, and falling asleep on an uncomfortable pew.

When I was eleven, I tried to convince someone God wasn't real. He made no difference to me!

Then I met a family who believed and trusted in God. They prayed, read the Bible and sang about Him; God was at the centre of their lives. As I spent time with them, I wondered if I was missing something. So when they invited me to church, I went.

I didn't have an amazing experience that suddenly convinced me the Bible was true. I went to church for two years, and there was lots I didn't understand. Often I went there to see my friends, but soon I loved being part of the church family.

Then I went on a Christian camp, and things I'd heard at church began to make sense. I understood Jesus died for me, because I needed forgiveness. He loved me, accepted me and wanted to be friends with me. I knew I had to say yes to following Jesus with my whole life!

Jo.

Dive in to the Bible

Think

What do you find hard about telling other people about Jesus?

Read 1 Peter 3 v 15-16

What two things are we told to do in verse 15?

1:

2:

If we "set apart Christ as Lord", it means Jesus is number one in our lives and we want to live for Him. When we believe He's in charge of everything, we'll want to pass the good news on… and tell people why we love Him and follow Him.

The "hope that you have" is the promise of forgiveness now and eternity with God.

Q: Why should we "always be prepared" to answer anyone who asks us about our hope?

Q: When might you have to give an answer?

You might be asked why you go to church, why you don't swear, or why you won't go out with someone who's not a Christian. Whatever the question, we should tell people we live the way we do because Jesus is Lord and we want to live for Him!

Q: How should we do it?

   1: (see end of v 15)

   2: (see v 16)

Earlier in this chapter we mentioned talking about Jesus, like Jesus and because of Jesus. If we ask Him, God will help us be gentle and respectful, and wise about what we say and how we say it. We want Jesus to be the big news, not us.

Pray

O Give thanks for the hope that Christians have.

O Pray that Christ would be number one in your life.

O Ask God to help you tell people about Jesus.

8. It's tough being true

Your relationship with the world

Imagine you suddenly landed on planet earth, and knew nothing about it! How long do you think it would be before you heard anything about God, or the name of Jesus mentioned?

It's easy to go for a day, week or longer without hearing about Jesus at all, or to only hear God's name used as a swear word. Many people ignore Jesus and aren't interested in knowing Him. They only seem interested in doing what they want and making sure they're happy.

It can be hard to follow Jesus in a world that doesn't have time for Him, doesn't think He's important and doesn't want to know Him.

Last Christmas I was given a box of ideas: "50 things to do once in a lifetime". Fifty things everyone should experience, such as:

O Take a boat trip whale watching

O Milk a cow

O Ride a camel in the desert

O Learn a foreign language

O Buy a metal detector and look for a hidden treasure

I've only done 13 of the 50; I still have a long way to go! But do you know that none of the ideas mentioned God? Not one of them suggested finding out why we're here or investigating if there's more to life than simply having fun and travelling around the world.

What are you here for?

Are you just here to do as many fun things as you can before you die?

What if you get to the end of your life and haven't married and had children, or become famous, or had a great job and earned lots of money? Does that mean you've wasted your life?

What can you hope to achieve in your lifetime? How can you make an impact in the world even if you never the leave the town you live in now?

We can just go through life crossing experiences off a list, such as:

O Have a boyfriend

O Travel the world

O Go to university

O Get a job

O Get married

O Have a baby

But there's a big chance we'd get to the end of our life and wonder what the point was—especially if we end up with lots of things we haven't done.

But there is a way to make sure we make the most of the life we have.

Do you want to live the best life possible?

Do you want to make the most of the days that you have here on earth?

Then read on…

Jesus said:

> **"I have come that they may have life, and have it to the full."**
>
> *John 10 v 10*

If you want to make the most of this life, the Bible says **we need Jesus**. Jesus came to earth as a man so we could have life.

We are called to "know Jesus, love Jesus and share Jesus".

Be holy... in an unholy world

In the earlier chapters we've seen how God calls us to be holy. He wants us to live the life He created us to live.

God wants you to be blameless and holy. That means knowing...

O God made you who you are—for a reason (Chapter 1).

O a relationship with God is essential (Chapter 2).

O meeting with God's family helps us grow (Chapter 3).

O being a good friend and having good friends helps us (Chapter 4).

O obeying our parents shows that we're living for God (Chapter 5).

O our attitude towards love and sex affects that (Chapter 6).

O we need to pass on the good news about Jesus (Chapter 7).

These things aren't easy, but they are how God wants His children to live.

Philippians 2 v 14-15 says:

Do everything without complaining or arguing, so that you may become blameless and pure, children of God without fault in a crooked and depraved generation.

Our world is described as "a crooked and depraved generation". That means people are sinful: they ignore God and do whatever they want—and sadly this is often dishonest and bad.

That's not a nice thing to hear, but think about the people around you. There will be people you know, or on TV/films, or in the news, who live as if they're in charge of everything. There are many people

who never think about God or that this is His world. Even Christians who love and follow God sometimes behave like this too.

What can we do?

In a world where God is often forgotten, and people think they're in charge, what can we do? Christians have a God-given responsibility to care for the world and the people living in it. This is an amazing planet—varied, exciting, and full of life. God put human beings in charge of looking after it in the way He says is best (Genesis 1 v 28). **Christians must care for the world and the people living in it.** There are many ways we can do that—things like:

O being a friend to the lonely

O teaching and caring for others

O picking up litter and recycling, caring for the world God has given us

O travelling to other countries to help people whose lives have been made difficult by sin in the world

Caring for others, showing them God's love and looking after God's creation should be something Christians love to do.

Whether we're…

O at home or at school

O out with our friends or on our own

O on holiday or in our home town

…if we trust in Jesus, wherever we are and whatever we're doing, we should be living to bring glory to God, living His way and being holy.

So, whether you eat or drink or whatever you do, do it all for the glory of God.

1 Corinthians 10 v 31

That means thinking of God first, not making ourselves look good. It means using what we do to show others how great God is.

Shine like stars

Do everything without complaining or arguing, so that you may become blameless and pure, children of God without fault in a crooked and depraved generation, in which you shine like stars in the universe as you hold out the word of life.

Philippians 2 v 14-16

Do you remember the embarrassing orange motor caravan my dad had? Well, he didn't just humiliate me by taking me to school in it; we also went on holiday in it. One year we had a holiday in East Germany (today there's only one Germany, but for a long time after World War 2 it was split into two countries.) In East Germany nearly everyone had the same small car, called a Trabant.

One evening we arrived at a new campsite. It was early evening, and still warm and sunny, so everyone was outside their tent or caravan, barbequing, having their dinner or playing games. Dad drove into the campsite, and my brother and I walked alongside the van. As we did, EVERYONE stopped what they were doing to look at us. People put down their barbeque tongs, their spoons and forks, their footballs and volleyballs to stare at this bright orange van driving through the field.

There was no missing it. We stuck out because no one else had anything like it! We couldn't have looked more different. Everyone knew about it, and as we drove on by, everyone was talking about it. I was quite relieved to finally park up and be able to hide inside! **We stood out because we were so different.**

Sometimes being different from everyone else can be hard. But Paul says that Christians should stand out; they should "shine like stars in the universe".

In a world where many people ignore God and do their own thing, Christians are called to stand out and be different. Our orange van was obvious for the entire campsite to see. Christians are told to shine for the entire world to see.

This doesn't mean deliberately being weird! But if we live God's way, people will notice.

If you call yourself a Christian, you can't sit back and blend in with everyone else. You can't ignore people in need. You can't keep Jesus just for Sunday and ignore Him the rest of the week. You are called to "shine like stars", so that people who don't believe in Him see you shining, and are challenged to think about Jesus.

How can you shine like a star? Here are some ideas:

O Not joining in with gossip when everyone else does

O Being friendly to the girl in class who not many people like

O Going to a school Christian group, even if others think you're weird

O Missing an outing with your friends, because you're helping a lady at church clear out her garden

O Obeying your parents, even when you find their rules hard

O Not watching a film / reading a book / listening to a song that doesn't respect God and the way He wants us to live

O Thinking more carefully about how you use the internet

The web

The internet is amazing—you can find out almost anything you want! There are facts it can teach us, things that will entertain us, and ways we can communicate with friends. It's a good way for people to stay in touch. However, it's all too easy to forget that what happens on the internet affects our real face-to-face friendships.

Maybe you fall out with a friend and then write something about them online. Many people can see it and get involved in an argument that was just between you and your friend. Before long it's become much bigger, and very hurtful things have been said.

Sometimes, people will type things they'd never say to a person's face—and then it's there, and can be read over and over again. Unkind words can be very painful.

Do you shine like a star when you're on the internet? If you're using it to continue arguments and hurt people, you need to think again. How can you use it to build up your friends, to encourage people and share Jesus' love?

But shining like stars is more than just doing good things. It's not about being noticed and everyone thinking you're a lovely person. The verse says: "shine like stars … as you hold out the word of life". People need to know **we're doing these things because of Jesus**, because we want to shine for Him. We want other people to come to know Him and have life "to the full" (John 10 v 10)—life the way Jesus intended. That means life here and now with Him as Lord, and when we die, life forever with God.

There are many girls today who are unhappy with the person they are. Some develop eating disorders, some hurt themselves, some don't respect themselves and end up in relationships that hurt them. **Jesus doesn't want that.** If we know that life with Jesus is how life is supposed to be, we can shine like stars and hold out the truth of Jesus to people who need it, people whose lives are missing the word of life.

Will you shine for Jesus and hold out the word of life through all you say and do? Will you show the world that knowing Jesus, loving Jesus and sharing Jesus is the best way to live the one life you have here on earth?

7 ideas to help you

1. ***Do you shine like a star when you're on the internet?*** If you're using facebook or something like it, or commenting on people's blogs or websites, does the language you use and the links you post show people you're "shining for Jesus"?

2. ***Does what you read / watch / listen to help you shine for Jesus?*** Do you just read / watch / listen to the same stuff as all your friends, or do you consider what the books are about, the theme of the film, or the words of the song? Are some of these things making it harder for you to shine for Jesus?

3. ***Does the way you spend your spare time help you shine for Jesus?*** Do you make time to regularly read your Bible and pray to God? Is church and/or youth group a priority, or do other things push them out?

4. ***What are you good at?*** What do you want to be when you grow older? It's great to have dreams and ambitions, and it's brilliant to think about how you can use and develop things you're good at. Are you excited about them bringing glory to you, making you look brilliant, and everyone praising you? Or are you excited about how you can use your gifts to bring glory to God—shining like a star for Him?

5. ***How can you shine at school?*** Would people know you were trying to live for Jesus from the way that you act in class, and speak to teachers, classmates and friends?

6. When people are in trouble or want advice, ***are you a person they come to***, because they know you're shining for Jesus and trying to love and care for people?

7. One star in the sky doesn't stand out as much as 50, 500, 5000 or 50,000 stars. ***Can you encourage other Christians you know to shine for Jesus, so that you can shine together?*** And invite other people to come to know and love Jesus, too?

True story: Imogen

I grew up in a vicarage, so Jesus was talked about a lot! I learned lots about the Bible and that following Jesus is the only way to know God and have the best life. I knew it, but always wondered if I was missing something.

I had friends who weren't Christians. I started to hang out with them more, and join in with what they did. I wanted to experiment and enjoy the world. But it wasn't as easy as I thought; doing these things didn't make me happy.

I still went to church and listened to God's Word, which wasn't easy. But it meant I was regularly reminded that living for Jesus is the best way. Nothing in this world is like Jesus. The world didn't send its son to die for me. The world doesn't care what happens in my life. I can't pray to the world or call it "Father". But it's easy to believe all the things the world offers are brilliant!

God helps me remember that Jesus died for me, and promises one day I'll be with Him forever. Life can be hard. I'm tempted to turn away from God sometimes—but God always forgives me.

Imogen
x

Dive in to the Bible

Think

What are some of the things you'd like to do in your lifetime?

O Go to university?

O Get married?

O Travel the world?

O Have a baby?

O Be famous?

O Be a missionary?

O Be really good at .... (sport/music/etc.)?

O Get a job as a ....?

O Something else?

Q: What does 1 Corinthians 10 v 31 remind us that we should do?

Doing everything for the glory of God means wanting God to be praised, not you. We can bring glory to God when we dry the dishes, tidy our rooms, chat to friends—even walk down the street!

Read Philippians 2 v 14-16

Christians are called to "shine like stars" in the world.

Q: Where do you find it easy to shine for Jesus?

Q: Where do you find it hard to shine?

Pray

Ask Jesus to help you "shine like a star" wherever you are, even when it's hard.

Q: How could you do that...

O at school?

O at home?

O with your friends?

O when life is difficult?

O when life is good?

Sometimes we don't feel like shining—life is hard, people hurt us or we just can't be bothered!

Q: What does verse 16 tell us we're "holding out"?

That means that even when things are difficult, we still have the amazing "word of life". Even when we're feeling at our lowest, God is with us and we have great news to share. With God's help we can keep shining for Him.

Pray

O Give thanks that even when things are tricky, you have the word of life—Jesus is always with you.

O Ask God to help you to shine like a star in the places you go to, and share the good news of Jesus with others.

Final thoughts

This is the end of the book. I hope and pray it has encouraged you, challenged you and made you think. I hope you'll keep dipping back into it and be reminded of how amazing Jesus is. I hope you'll see that knowing and loving Jesus affects EVERY relationship you have, and everything you do, say and think.

As you live in a world where many people get their advice and wisdom from magazines, self-help books, films and TV shows, remember that God has written down all that we need to know to live for Him. It's all together in one book, the Bible!

Keep going!

Paul wrote a letter to Timothy, who was younger than him, encouraging him to keep going as a Christian. He reminds Timothy that he knows the truth—people have taught it to him and he's read it in the Bible. Knowing this truth means he can be in a relationship with God.

But as for you, continue in what you have learned and have become convinced of, because you know those from whom you learned it, and how from infancy you have known the holy Scriptures, which are able to make you wise for salvation through faith in Christ Jesus. All Scripture is God-breathed and is useful for teaching, rebuking, correcting and training in righteousness, so that the man of God may be thoroughly equipped for every good work.

2 Timothy 3 v 14-17

The Bible is so important because it's "God-breathed"—the words come from God Himself. So keep reading it; it contains all you need to know and love Jesus. As you read it, you will get to know God better.

O God's Word teaches us (about who He is and what He's done).

O It rebukes us (shows us where we're going wrong).

O It corrects us (shows us the right way to go).

O It trains us in righteousness (helps us to be holy and live for God).

The Bible will help us to live for Him in this world, whatever we're doing.

Read it regularly

I'm not very good in the morning. In fact I'm a bit of a "grunter"—someone who struggles to talk until they've had a shower and eaten some breakfast! When I was younger, I used to get up and grunt at both my mum and dad on the way to the bathroom, and they would smile and nod back.

They didn't start a conversation with me—not because I was a grunter, but because they were both reading their Bible. My mum read in bed, and my dad read downstairs in an armchair. **Nearly every morning I'd get up and see them reading the Bible.** They helped to show me just how important it is to read God's Word. It will help me live in a place where so many people don't put God first.

I try to read my Bible every day (after a shower and breakfast so I'm more awake!). I don't always manage it, but I do try and make it a priority. I want to make sure that as I live in the world, I'm listening to God, I'm hearing His wisdom, and following His way of life instead of listening to the lies of the world.

If you're a morning person, you could try and read the Bible when you wake up, or straight after breakfast. If you're an evening person, you might find it easier before you go to bed. Many people find it helps to do it at the same time each day, so you get into a pattern. It's good to find a quiet spot, where other people won't disturb you and you won't be distracted by the TV, internet or your phone!

Some people follow a plan, reading a couple of chapters a day. Bible-reading notes can be helpful (they're mentioned at the end of chapter 2, page 23). You could also re-read what your church or youth group are studying to help you remember it.

This might be a helpful plan:

O Choose a time that works for you.

O Find a quiet place to read.

O Pray, asking God to help you understand what you read, and learn from it.

O Read the Bible, and your notes if you have them, and think about what you've read.

O Pray:

- Praise and thank God for what you've learned.

- Ask Him to help you put it into practice.

- Say sorry for not living for Him.

- Pray for other people and situations around the world.

- Pray for yourself.

True life

I'm fairly certain I'm never going to appear in a blockbuster film, or be a TV presenter. I won't travel round the world in a girl band, or become a millionaire. There will be millions of people in the world who'll never have any idea who I am.

But I know that, at the end of my life, I will be able to look back and say: *I was forgiven by Jesus, and I tried to live for Him every day*. I mess up, I let God down, I don't get everything right—but with God's help I will keep following Him.

I want to be able to say my life counted, because my life was lived for God.

Will you be able to say the same thing about yours?

Thanks!

I would like to dedicate this book to:

Ellie,

and Naomi, Lydia, and Beth.

A big thank you to:

O Laura, Phoebe, Jessica, Rhema, Chloe and Charlotte for reading chapters, telling me you enjoyed it, and wanting to read more.

O Rachael, Sarah, Dawn, Mel, Penny, Pip, Pete, Paul, my family (Mum, Dad, David, Jon, Rebecca, Sarah, Ellie, Ben and Sam) and others who have challenged and encouraged me as I wrote it.

O And all the 11-14 year-old girls I've had the privilege of working with at Pathfinder camp (Bideford, Shaftesbury, Southwold, Barnstaple and Casterton), at Keswick week 1, and those from St Peter's, Harold Wood; Grace Church, Muswell Hill; and Holy Trinity Platt, Manchester.

O And a special thanks to André Parker for the fantastic cartoons, Alison Mitchell for encouraging me to keep writing, and all the wonderful people at The Good Book Company.

Telling your friends about Jesus

Do you find it hard to tell your friends about Jesus? Here's some online stuff that will help you.

O Go to **www.thegoodbook.co.uk/true** to download a sheet full of great ideas to help you talk to your friends about Jesus. Read them through, choose one or two you think will help your friends, ask God to help you—and go for it!

O *Who will be King?* is a simple explanation of why God is the Real King of everyone and everything, and how we can know Him as our Friend, Father and King. You can find this online at **www.matthiasmedia.com.au/2wtl/whowillbeking**

Or you can buy the booklet from any of our websites:

UK & Europe: www.thegoodbook.co.uk
North America: www.thegoodbook.com
Australia: www.thegoodbook.com.au
New Zealand: www.thegoodbook.co.nz

O And finally… you can watch a cartoon explaining who Jesus is and why He came at **www.christianityexplored.org/what-is-christianity**

Perhaps you could watch this with a friend and then talk about it afterwards. (Watch it yourself first to check if your friend would find it helpful.)

Dive in to the Bible

Have you enjoyed diving in to the Bible? Don't stop now!

Discover

Discover notes are **a great way to start reading the Bible.** They're full of puzzles, prayers, pondering points and weird words.

"*Discover... God's amazing word*" is a 3-week starter issue where you can meet Jesus in Mark's Gospel, discover some brilliant stuff about God's word from the book of psalms, and use your **free bookmark** to see how the Bible fits together.

Engage

For those who want to **get stuck into the Bible in a deeper way.** Great questions and help for understanding God's book.

If you collect them for long enough, your *Engage* copies will make a whole library that helps you dive in to all 66 books of the Bible. Amazing!

You can hunt down *Discover* or *Engage*, plus some other great books to help you grow as a follower of Jesus, at any of The Good Book Company websites (page 128).

LOST

When the Dream turns to a Nightmare

A son turns his back on home and family to follow his dreams of a new life on his own. Another son stays dutifully at home.

But **when the dream turns to a nightmare**, what will this first son do? And which of the two sons is really the more lost?

In this deceptively simple story, Jesus gets to the heart of what it means to be lost to God, and found by him again. And it's a story that's **full of surprises**.

You'll be surprised by the father, surprised by the sons, and surprised by what this story tells us about our own hearts.

And there there's the biggest surprise of all...

Jaw-dropping in fact...

UK & Europe: www.thegoodbook.co.uk
North America: www.thegoodbook.com
Australia: www.thegoodbook.com.au
New Zealand: www.thegoodbook.co.nz